Cambridge Latin Course

Book I

FOURTH EDITION

CAMBRIDGE
UNIVERSITY PRESS

CAMBRIDGE
UNIVERSITY PRESS

University Printing House, Cambridge CB2 8BS, United Kingdom

Cambridge University Press is part of the University of Cambridge.

It furthers the University's mission by disseminating knowledge in the pursuit of education, learning and research at the highest international levels of excellence.

Information on this title: education.cambridge.org

This book, an outcome of work jointly commissioned by the Schools Council before its closure and the Cambridge School Classics Project, is published under the aegis of Qualifications and Curriculum Authority Enterprises Limited, Newcombe House, 45 Notting Hill Gate, London W11 3JB

First published 1970
Second edition 1982
Integrated edition 1990
Fourth edition 1998
24th printing 2014

Printed in the United Kingdom by Latimer Trend

A catalogue record for this publication is available from the British Library

ISBN 978-0-521-63543-1 Paperback

Cover photographs by R. L. Dalladay
Maps and plans by Robert Calow / Eikon
Illustrations by Joy Mellor and Leslie Jones

ACKNOWLEDGEMENTS

Thanks are due to the following for permision to reproduce photographs:

p. 14 *all images*, p. 79 *br*, p. 109 *bl*, p. 139, p. 161, © British Museum; p. 15, The Metropolitan Museum of Art, Rogers Fund, 1903 (03.14.13). Photograph by Schecter Lee. Photograph © 1986 The Metropolitan Museum of Art; p. 21, p. 25 *cl*, p. 37 *tl*, p. 51 *no.* 10, p. 94 *bl* and *br*, p. 105, p. 109 *tr [neck guard]* and *br [greave]*, p. 122, p. 123, p. 124, p 125 *no.* 3, p. 128, p. 177, Cambridge School Classics Project; p. 44 *tc*, p. 167 *r*, Courtesy of the Trustees of the V & A; p. 44 *l* © The Fitzwilliam Museum, University of Cambridge; p. 51 *br* reproduced from *The Gardens of Pompeii* by W. F. Jashemsky (Caratzas Brothers, New Rochelle, NY); p. 67 *tl* and *bl* Visual Publications; p. 69, Musée royal de Mariemont (Morlanwelz, Belgique); p. 129, Giraudon; p. 141, by permission of The British Library, MS 34286 (1); p. 174 *b* and *br*, O. Louis Mazzatenta / National Geographic Image Collection.

Thanks are due to the Museo Archeologico Nazionale, Naples, for permission to reproduce images on p. 9 *cl* and *br*, p. 10 *r*, p. 47 *r*, p. 58 and p. 76.

Other photography by R. L. Dalladay.

Contents

CAECILIUS

STAGE 1

Caecilius

familia

1 Caecilius est pater.

2 Metella est māter.

3 Quīntus est fīlius.

5 Grumiō est coquus.

4 Clēmēns est servus.

6 Cerberus est canis.

7 Caecilius est in tablīnō.

8 Metella est in ātriō.

9 Quīntus est in triclīniō.

10 Clēmēns est in hortō.

11 Grumiō est in culīnā.

12 Cerberus est in viā.

13 pater est in tablīnō.
   pater in tablīnō scrībit.

14 māter est in ātriō.
   māter in ātriō sedet.

15 fīlius est in triclīniō.
   fīlius in triclīniō bibit.

16 servus est in hortō.
   servus in hortō labōrat.

17 coquus est in culīnā.
   coquus in culīnā labōrat.

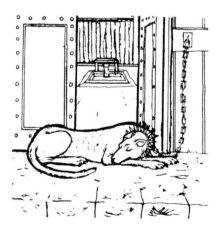

18 canis est in viā.
   canis in viā dormit.

Vocabulary

est	*is*	in tablīnō	*in the study*	scrībit	*is writing*
pater	*father*	in ātriō	*in the atrium*	sedet	*is sitting*
māter	*mother*		*(main room)*	bibit	*is drinking*
fīlius	*son*	in triclīniō	*in the dining-*	labōrat	*is working*
servus	*slave*		*room*	dormit	*is sleeping*
coquus	*cook*	in hortō	*in the garden*		
canis	*dog*	in culīnā	*in the kitchen*		
		in viā	*in the street*		

Cerberus

Caecilius est in hortō. Caecilius in hortō sedet. servus est in ātriō. servus in ātriō labōrat. Metella est in ātriō. Metella in ātriō sedet. Quīntus est in tablīnō. Quīntus in tablīnō scrībit. Cerberus est in viā.

Caecilius had this mosaic of a dog in the doorway of his house.

intrat *enters*
circumspectat *looks round*
cibus *food*
in mēnsā *on the table*
salit *jumps*
stat *stands*
stertit *snores*
lātrat *barks*
surgit *gets up*
īrātus *angry*
pestis! *pest!*
furcifer! *scoundrel!*
clāmat *shouts*
exit *goes out*

coquus est in culīnā. coquus in culīnā dormit. Cerberus intrat. Cerberus circumspectat. cibus est in mēnsā. canis salit. canis in mēnsā stat. Grumiō stertit. canis lātrat. Grumiō surgit. coquus est īrātus. 'pestis! furcifer!' coquus clāmat. Cerberus exit.

5

About the language

1   Latin sentences containing the word **est** often have the same order as English. For example:

> Metella est māter.
> *Metella is the mother.*
>
> canis est in viā.
> *The dog is in the street.*

2   In other Latin sentences, the order is usually different from that of English. For example:

> canis in viā dormit.
> *The dog is sleeping in the street.*
>
> servus in culīnā labōrat.
> *The slave is working in the kitchen.*

3   Note that **dormit** and **labōrat** in the sentences above can be translated in another way. For example: **servus in culīnā labōrat** can mean *The slave works in the kitchen* as well as *The slave is working in the kitchen.* The story will help you to decide which translation gives the better sense.

Practising the language

Write out each Latin sentence, completing it with a suitable word or phrase from the box. Then translate the sentence. Use each word or phrase only once.

> For example: . . . . est in hortō.
> **servus** est in hortō.
> *The slave is in the garden.*

1	Quīntus	Grumiō	Caecilius
	canis	māter	servus

2	in viā	in hortō	in ātriō
	in tablīnō	in culīnā	in triclīniō

1
a   . . . . est in hortō.
b   . . . . est in viā.
c   . . . . est in culīnā.
d   . . . . est in tablīnō.
e   . . . . est in ātriō.
f   . . . . est in triclīniō.

2
a   Clēmēns . . . . labōrat.
b   Caecilius . . . . scrībit.
c   canis . . . . lātrat.
d   Metella . . . . stat.
e   coquus est . . . .
f   Quīntus est . . . .

Caecilius

Caecilius lived in Italy during the first century A.D. in the town of Pompeii. The town was situated at the foot of Mount Vesuvius on the coast of the Bay of Naples, and may have had a population of about 10,000. Caecilius was a rich Pompeian banker. When archaeologists excavated his house they discovered his accounts in a strong-box. These documents tell us that he was also an auctioneer, tax-collector, farmer and money-lender.

He inherited some of his money, but he probably made most of it through shrewd and energetic business activities. He dealt in slaves, cloth, timber and property. He also ran a laundry and dyeing business, grazed sheep and cattle on pastureland outside the town, and he sometimes won the contract for collecting the local taxes. He may have owned a few shops as well, and probably lent money to local shipping companies wishing to trade with countries overseas. The profit on such trading was often very large.

Caecilius' full name was Lucius Caecilius Iucundus. Lucius was his personal name, rather like a modern first name. His second name, Caecilius, shows that he was a member of the

The front of Caecilius' house. The spaces on either side of the door were shops he probably owned.

A laundry like this was among his business interests.

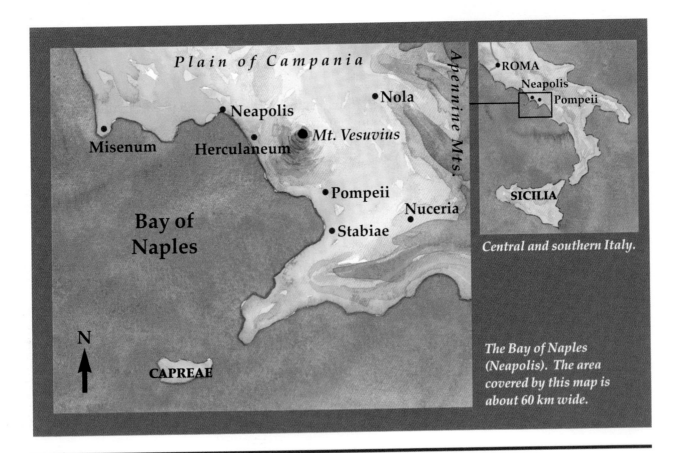

Central and southern Italy.

The Bay of Naples (Neapolis). The area covered by this map is about 60 km wide.

'clan' of the Caecilii. Clans or groups of families were very important and strong feelings of loyalty existed within them. Caecilius' third name, Iucundus, is the name of his own family and close relatives. The word **iūcundus** means 'pleasant' just as in English we find surnames like Merry or Jolly.

Only a Roman citizen would have three names. A slave would have just one, such as Clemens or Grumio. As a Roman citizen, Caecilius not only had the right to vote in elections, but also was fully protected by the law against unjust treatment. The slaves who lived and worked in his house and in his businesses had no rights of their own. They were his property and he could treat them well or badly as he wished. There was one important exception to this rule. The law did not allow a master to put a slave to death without showing good reason.

This head found in Caecilius' house may be a portrait of him.

Roman coins: a bronze sestertius, a silver denarius and a gold aureus.

Below: *Caecilius kept his tablets and money in a wood and metal strong-box like this.*

This is one of the wooden tablets found in Caecilius' house. They recorded his business dealings. The writing was on wax in the central recess and when the tablets were discovered much of the writing could still be read. The tablets were tied together in twos or threes through the holes at the top.

One page of the writing: it records the sale at auction of a slave for 6,252 sesterces.

Metella

Caecilius' wife Metella, like many Roman wives and mothers, had an important position in her home. She was responsible for the management of the household, and had to supervise the work of the domestic slaves. In order to run the house successfully she would need to be well organised, and firm but sensitive in her control of the slaves. She would also supervise preparations for social occasions and help her husband to entertain guests.

Although their lives were mainly centred on their homes, married women would go out to visit friends, to shop, and to attend public events. Occasionally they managed their own businesses, although this was not common.

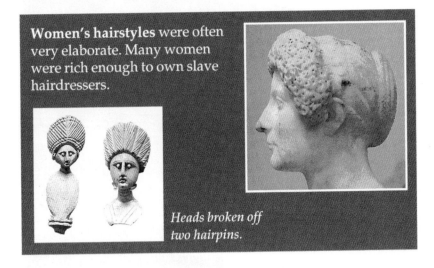

Women's hairstyles were often very elaborate. Many women were rich enough to own slave hairdressers.

Heads broken off two hairpins.

Eumachia, a Pompeian business woman who built the Clothworkers' Guildhall in the forum.

Houses in Pompeii

The house in which a wealthy man like Caecilius lived differed in several ways from an equivalent house today. The house came right up to the pavement; there was no garden or grass in front of it. The windows were few, small and placed fairly high up. They were intended to let in enough light, but to keep out the heat of the sun. Large windows would have made the rooms uncomfortably hot in summer and cold in winter.

Most houses stood only one storey high, although some had a second floor above. Many had shops on either side of the main door, which were rented out by the owner of the house. From the outside, with its few windows and high walls stretching all the way round, the house did not look very attractive or inviting.

Plan of a Pompeian house

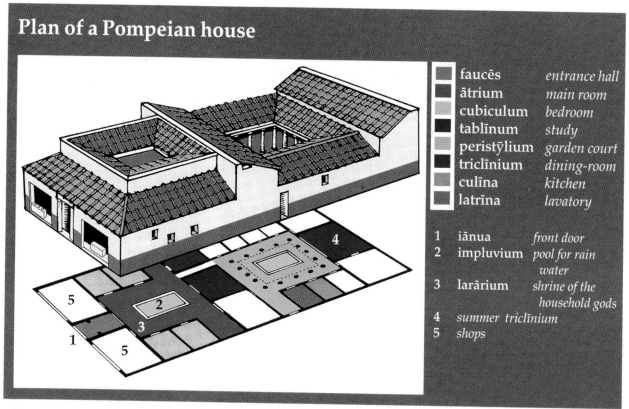

	faucēs	*entrance hall*
	ātrium	*main room*
	cubiculum	*bedroom*
	tablīnum	*study*
	peristȳlium	*garden court*
	triclīnium	*dining-room*
	culīna	*kitchen*
	latrīna	*lavatory*

1   iānua   *front door*
2   impluvium   *pool for rain water*
3   larārium   *shrine of the household gods*
4   *summer triclīnium*
5   *shops*

The ground plan of the house shows two parts or areas of about equal size. They look like courtyards surrounded by rooms opening off the central space. Let us examine these two parts more closely.

The main entrance to the house was on the side facing the street. It consisted of a tall double door. The Latin word for this door was **iānua**. On passing through the door, the visitor came into a short corridor which led straight into the main room, the **ātrium**. This impressive room, which was used for important family occasions and for receiving visitors, was large and high and contained little furniture. The roof sloped down slightly towards a large square opening in the middle. The light streamed in through the opening high overhead. Immediately below was the **impluvium**, a shallow rectangular pool, lined with marble, which collected the rain water.

One of the most striking things about the atrium was the sense of space. The high roof with the glimpse of the sky through the central opening, the large floor area and the absence of much furnishing all helped to give this impression. The furniture would include a bronze or marble table, a couch, and perhaps a strong-box in which the family valuables were stored. In a corner, near the main door, was the **larārium**, a small shrine at which the family gods were worshipped. The floor of the atrium was paved with marble slabs or sometimes with mosaics.

In what ways is this house typical of houses in Caecilius' day?

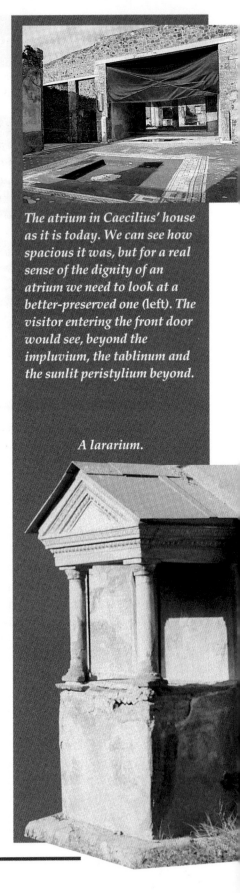

The atrium in Caecilius' house as it is today. We can see how spacious it was, but for a real sense of the dignity of an atrium we need to look at a better-preserved one (left). The visitor entering the front door would see, beyond the impluvium, the tablinum and the sunlit peristylium beyond.

A lararium.

The walls were decorated with panels of brightly painted plaster. The Pompeians were especially fond of red, orange and blue. On many of these panels there were scenes from well-known stories, especially the Greek myths.

Round the atrium were arranged the bedrooms, study and dining-room. The entrances to these rooms were usually provided not with a wooden door but with a heavy curtain.

From this first area of the house, the visitor walked through the **tablīnum** (study), or a passage, into the second part. This was the **peristȳlium**, which was made up of a colonnade of pillars surrounding the **hortus** (garden). Like the atrium, the colonnade was often elaborately decorated. Around the outside of the colonnade were the summer dining-room, kitchen, lavatory, slaves' quarters and storage rooms. Some houses also had their own set of baths.

The garden was laid out with flowers and shrubs in a careful plan. In the small fish-pond in the middle, a fountain threw up a jet of water, and marble statues of gods and heroes stood here and there. In the peristylium, the members of the family enjoyed the sunshine or shade as they wished; here they relaxed on their own or entertained their guests.

The Pompeians not only lived in houses that looked very different from modern ones, but also thought very differently about them. They did not expect their houses to be private places restricted to the family and close friends. Instead, the master conducted much of his business and social life from home. He would receive and do business with most visitors in the atrium. The more important ones would be invited into the tablinum. Certain very close business friends and high-ranking individuals would receive invitations to dine or relax in the peristylium with the family.

Even if there were no outsiders present, the members of the family were never on their own. They were surrounded and often outnumbered by their slaves. They did not attach as much importance to privacy as many people do today.

Only the wealthy lived like this; most people lived in much simpler homes. Some of the poorer shopkeepers, for instance, would have had only a room or two above their shops. In large cities such as Rome, many people lived in blocks of flats several storeys high, some of them in very poor conditions.

Caecilius' tablinum was decorated with a particularly expensive shade of red paint – now mostly perished.

A painting of a marble fountain in a garden.

A peristylium, with hanging ornaments between the columns.

Vocabulary checklist 1

canis	dog
coquus	cook
est	is
fīlius	son
hortus	garden
in	in
labōrat	works, is working
māter	mother
pater	father
sedet	sits, is sitting
servus	slave
via	street

Metella was very fond of jewellery. Here are some examples of the things she might have worn.

IN VILLA

STAGE 2

amīcus

1 Caecilius est in ātriō.

2 amīcus Caecilium salūtat.

3 Metella est in ātriō.

4 amīcus Metellam salūtat.

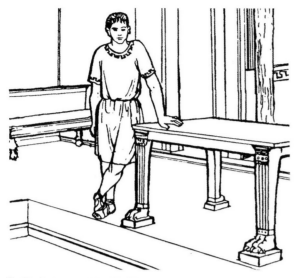

5 Quīntus est in ātriō.

6 amīcus Quīntum salūtat.

7 servus est in ātriō.

8 amīcus servum salūtat.

9 canis est in ātriō.

10 amīcus canem salūtat.

Metella

11 coquus est in culīnā.

12 Metella culīnam intrat.

13 Grumiō labōrat.

14 Metella Grumiōnem spectat.

15 cibus est parātus.

16 Metella cibum gustat.

17 Grumiō est anxius.

18 Metella Grumiōnem laudat.

19 amīcus est in hortō.

20 Metella amīcum vocat.

mercātor

mercātor *merchant*

amīcus Caecilium vīsitat. amīcus est mercātor. mercātor vīllam
intrat. Clēmēns est in ātriō. Clēmēns mercātōrem salūtat.
Caecilius est in tablīnō. Caecilius pecūniam numerat. Caecilius
est argentārius. amīcus tablīnum intrat. Caecilius surgit.

'salvē!' Caecilius mercātōrem salūtat.   5

'salvē!' mercātor respondet.

Caecilius triclīnium intrat. amīcus quoque intrat. amīcus in
lectō recumbit. argentārius in lectō recumbit.

Grumiō in culīnā cantat. Grumiō pāvōnem coquit. coquus est
laetus. Caecilius coquum audit. Caecilius nōn est laetus.   10
Caecilius cēnam exspectat. amīcus cēnam exspectat. Caecilius
Grumiōnem vituperat.

amīcus *friend*
vīsitat *is visiting*
vīllam *house*
salūtat *greets*
pecūniam
  numerat *is counting money*
argentārius *banker*
salvē! *hello!*
respondet *replies*
quoque *also*
in lectō recumbit *reclines on
              a couch*
cantat *is singing*
pāvōnem *peacock*
coquit *is cooking*
laetus *happy*
audit *hears*
nōn est *is not*
cēnam *dinner*
exspectat *is waiting for*
vituperat *blames, curses*

in triclīniō

Grumiō triclīnium intrat. Grumiō pāvōnem portat. Clēmēns
triclīnium intrat. Clēmēns vīnum portat. Caecilius pāvōnem
gustat.

'pāvō est optimus!' Caecilius clāmat.

mercātor quoque pāvōnem gustat. mercātor cēnam laudat.   5
dominus coquum laudat. Grumiō exit.

ancilla intrat. ancilla suāviter cantat. ancilla dominum
dēlectat. ancilla mercātōrem dēlectat. mox dominus dormit.
amīcus quoque dormit.

Grumiō triclīnium intrat et circumspectat. coquus cibum in   10
mēnsā videt. Grumiō cibum cōnsūmit et vīnum bibit! Caecilius
Grumiōnem nōn videt. coquus in triclīniō magnificē cēnat.

coquus ancillam spectat. ancilla Grumiōnem dēlectat.
Grumiō ancillam dēlectat. Grumiō est laetissimus.

portat *is carrying*
vīnum *wine*
gustat *tastes*
optimus *very good, excellent*
laudat *praises*
dominus *master*
ancilla *slave-girl, maid*
suāviter *sweetly*
dēlectat *pleases*
mox *soon*
et *and*
videt *sees*
cibum cōnsūmit *eats the food*
magnificē *magnificently,
         in style*
cēnat *dines, has dinner*
spectat *looks at*
laetissimus *very happy*

About the language

1   Words like **Metella, Caecilius** and **mercātor** are known as **nouns**.
    They often indicate people or animals (e.g. **ancilla** and **canis**), places
    (e.g. **vīlla, hortus**), and things (e.g. **cēna, cibus**).

2   You have now met two forms of the same noun:

      Metella – Metellam
      Caecilius – Caecilium
      mercātor – mercātōrem

3   The different forms are known as the **nominative case** and the
    accusative case.

nominative	Metella	Caecilius	mercātor
accusative	Metellam	Caecilium	mercātōrem

4   If Metella does something, such as praising Grumio,
    the nominative **Metella** is used:

      Metella Grumiōnem laudat.
      Metella praises Grumio.

5   But if somebody else does something to Metella,
    the accusative **Metellam** is used:

      amīcus **Metellam** salūtat.
      The friend greets Metella.

6   Notice again the difference in word order
    between Latin and English:

      coquus culīnam intrat.
      The cook enters the kitchen.

      Clēmēns vīnum portat.
      Clemens carries the wine.

*Peacocks often figured
on Pompeian wall-
paintings as well as
on their dinner tables.*

Practising the language

1   Write out each Latin sentence, completing it with a
    suitable word or phrase from the box. Then translate
    the sentence. Use each word or phrase only once.

    For example: canis . . . . stat.
                    canis **in viā** stat.
                    The dog is standing in the street.

scrībit	in culīnā
servus	amīcus
sedet	in viā

    a   Grumiō . . . . coquit.   d   Cerberus . . . . dormit.
    b   . . . . in hortō labōrat.   e   Metella in ātriō . . . .
    c   mercātor in tablīnō . . . . . .   f   . . . . in triclīniō cēnat.

2   Write out each Latin sentence, completing it with the right
    word from the brackets. Then translate the sentence.

    For example: amīcus Caecilium . . . . (sedet, vīsitat)
                    amīcus Caecilium **vīsitat**.
                    A friend visits Caecilius.

    a   Caecilius pecūniam . . . . (numerat, dormit)
    b   Clēmēns vīnum . . . . (labōrat, portat)
    c   ancilla hortum . . . . (intrat, gustat)
    d   Metella mercātōrem . . . . (salūtat, cantat)
    e   Quīntus cibum . . . . (vīsitat, cōnsūmit)
    f   servus vīllam . . . . (dormit, intrat, portat)
    g   amīcus Grumiōnem . . . . (spectat, stat, recumbit)
    h   māter fīlium . . . . (bibit, dormit, vituperat)
    i   mercātor canem . . . . (sedet, cōnsūmit, audit)
    j   dominus ancillam . . . . (scrībit, laudat, numerat)

3   Translate this story:

amīcus

amīcus Grumiōnem vīsitat. amīcus est servus. servus
vīllam intrat. Clēmēns est in ātriō. servus Clēmentem
videt. Clēmēns servum salūtat. servus culīnam intrat.
servus culīnam circumspectat.
   Grumiō nōn est in culīnā. servus cibum videt. cibus   5
est parātus! servus cibum gustat. cibus est optimus.   **parātus** *ready*
   Grumiō culīnam intrat. Grumiō amīcum videt.
amīcus cibum cōnsūmit! coquus est īrātus.
   'pestis! furcifer!' coquus clāmat. coquus amīcum
vituperat.   *10*

Daily life

The day began early for Caecilius and the members of his household. He would usually get up at dawn. His slaves were up even earlier, sweeping, dusting and polishing.

It did not take Caecilius long to dress. The first garment that he put on was his tunic, similar to a short-sleeved shirt, then his **toga**, a very large piece of woollen cloth arranged in folds, and finally his shoes, which were rather like modern sandals. A quick wash of the hands and face with cold water was enough at that time of the morning. Later he would visit a barber and be shaved, and in the afternoon he would enjoy a leisurely visit to the public baths.

His wife, Metella, also got up early. She would put on a **stola**, a full-length tunic. If she was going out, she would also wear a large rectangular shawl. With the help of a skilled slave-woman, she did her hair in the latest style, put on her make-up, including powder, rouge and mascara, and arranged her jewellery, of which she would have had a large and varied collection.

Breakfast was only a light snack, often just a cup of water and a piece of bread. The first duty of the day for Caecilius was to receive the respectful greetings of a number of poorer people and freedmen who had previously been his slaves. He would receive these visitors in the atrium and hand out small sums of money to them. If they were in any kind of trouble, he gave them as much help and protection as he could. In return, they helped Caecilius in several ways. For example, they accompanied him as a group of supporters on public occasions, and they might also be employed by him in business affairs. They were known as his **clientēs**, and he was their **patrōnus**. After seeing these visitors, if he had no further business to conduct at home, Caecilius set out for the **forum** (market-place), where he spent the rest of the morning trading and banking.

Lunch was eaten at about midday, and it was also a light meal. It usually consisted of some meat or fish followed by fruit. Business ended soon after lunch. Caecilius would then have a short siesta before going to the baths. Towards the end of the afternoon, the main meal of the day began. This was called **cēna**.

An important Roman dressed in his toga. This hot and unwieldy garment was valued because only citizens could wear it.

Bankers in the forum.

During the winter, the family used the inner dining-room near the atrium. In the summer, they would generally have preferred the dining-room at the back of the house, which looked straight out onto the garden. Three couches were arranged around a circular table which, though small, was very elegantly carved and decorated. Each couch had places for three people. The diners reclined on the couches, leaning on their left elbow and taking food from the table with their right hand. The food was cut up by a slave before being served, and diners ate it with their fingers or a spoon. Forks were not used by the Romans. Not all Romans reclined when eating dinner, but it was usual among rich or upper-class families. Poor people, slaves, children and sometimes women would eat sitting up.

The meal was not hurried, for this was an occasion to talk and relax over good food. If guests were invited, some form of entertainment was often provided.

This drawing shows how the couches were arranged in a Roman dining-room. The Latin name triclinium means a room with three couches.

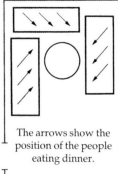

The arrows show the position of the people eating dinner.

A Roman dinner

The meal began with a first course of light dishes to whet the appetite. Eggs, fish, and cooked and raw vegetables were often served. Then came the main course in which a variety of meat dishes with different sauces and vegetables would be offered. Beef, pork, mutton and poultry were all popular, and in preparing them the cook would do his best to show off his skill and imagination. Finally, the dessert was brought in, consisting of fruit, nuts, cheese and sweet dishes. Wine produced locally from the vineyards on Vesuvius was drunk during the meal.

Many loaves of bread have been found in the ruins of Pompeii.

Roman dinners were said to run 'from eggs to apples'; this bowl of eggs has survived from Pompeii.

Fish and other seafood were much enjoyed.

Above and below: To round off the meal: the fruit bowl and the basket of figs.

Main course ingredients – a rabbit and a chicken – hanging in a larder.

Vocabulary checklist 2

amīcus	*friend*
ancilla	*slave-girl, maid*
cēna	*dinner*
cibus	*food*
dominus	*master*
dormit	*sleeps*
intrat	*enters*
laetus	*happy*
laudat	*praises*
mercātor	*merchant*
quoque	*also*
salūtat	*greets*

Grumio did most of his cooking with pans and grills over charcoal, like a barbecue.

NEGOTIUM

STAGE 3

in forō

Caecilius nōn est in vīllā. Caecilius in forō negōtium agit.
Caecilius est argentārius. argentārius pecūniam numerat.
    Caecilius forum circumspectat. ecce! pictor in forō ambulat.
pictor est Celer. Celer Caecilium salūtat.
    ecce! tōnsor quoque est in forō. tōnsor est Pantagathus.
Caecilius tōnsōrem videt.
    'salvē!' Caecilius tōnsōrem salūtat.
    'salvē!' Pantagathus respondet.
    ecce! vēnālīcius forum intrat. vēnālīcius est Syphāx.
vēnālīcius mercātōrem exspectat. mercātor nōn venit. Syphāx
est īrātus. Syphāx mercātōrem vituperat.

in forō *in the forum*

negōtium agit *is working,*
                       is doing business
ecce! *look!*
pictor *painter, artist*
5   **ambulat** *is walking*
tōnsor *barber*

vēnālīcius *slave-dealer*
10 **nōn venit** *does not come*

pictor

pictor ad vīllam venit. pictor est Celer. Celer iānuam pulsat.
Clēmēns pictōrem nōn audit. servus est in hortō. Celer clāmat.
canis Celerem audit et lātrat. Quīntus canem audit. Quīntus ad
iānuam venit. fīlius iānuam aperit. Celer Quīntum salūtat et
vīllam intrat.   5

Metella est in culīnā. Quīntus mātrem vocat. Metella ātrium
intrat. pictor Metellam salūtat. Metella pictōrem ad triclīnium dūcit.

Celer in triclīniō labōrat. Celer pictūram pingit. magnus leō
est in pictūrā. Herculēs quoque est in pictūrā. leō Herculem
ferōciter petit. Herculēs magnum fūstem tenet et leōnem   10
verberat. Herculēs est fortis.

Caecilius ad vīllam revenit et triclīnium intrat. Caecilius
pictūram intentē spectat et pictūram laudat.

ad vīllam *to the house*
iānuam pulsat *knocks at the door*
ad iānuam *to the door*
aperit *opens*
vocat *calls*
dūcit *leads, takes*
pictūram pingit *paints a picture*
magnus *big*
leō *lion*
ferōciter *fiercely*
petit *is going for, is attacking*
fūstem *club*
tenet *is holding*
verberat *is striking*
fortis *brave, strong*
revenit *returns*
intentē *closely, carefully*

Roman painters were often very skilled: (left to right) shepherd boy with pipes; a cupid catching a rabbit; a portrait, possibly of a poet.

tōnsor

When you have read this story, answer the questions at the end.
Answer in English unless you are asked for Latin.

tōnsor in tabernā labōrat. tōnsor est Pantagathus. Caecilius intrat.
   'salvē, tōnsor!' inquit Caecilius.
   'salvē!' respondet Pantagathus.
   tōnsor est occupātus. senex in sellā sedet. Pantagathus
novāculam tenet et barbam tondet. senex novāculam intentē   5
spectat.
   poēta tabernam intrat. poēta in tabernā stat et versum recitat.
versus est scurrīlis. Caecilius rīdet. sed tōnsor nōn rīdet. tōnsor
est īrātus.
   'furcifer! furcifer!' clāmat Pantagathus. senex est perterritus.   10
tōnsor barbam nōn tondet. tōnsor senem secat. multus
sanguis fluit.
   Caecilius surgit et ē tabernā exit.

Glossary	
in tabernā	*in the shop*
inquit	*says*
occupātus	*busy*
senex	*old man*
in sellā	*in the chair*
novāculam	*razor*
barbam tondet	*is trimming his beard*
poēta	*poet*
versum recitat	*recites a line, recites a verse*
scurrīlis	*rude*
rīdet	*laughs, smiles*
sed	*but*
perterritus	*terrified*
secat	*cuts*
multus	*much*
sanguis	*blood*
fluit	*flows*
ē tabernā	*out of the shop*

Questions

Marks

1 Who is working in the shop when Caecilius arrives?   1
2 **tōnsor est occupātus** (line 4). Look at the rest of the paragraph and say why the barber is described as busy.   1
3 In line 7, who else comes into the shop?   1
4 **Caecilius rīdet** (line 8). What makes Caecilius laugh?   1
5 In lines 8–9, what is the barber's reaction?   1
6 In line 11, what does the barber do to the old man?   1
7 What does Caecilius do at the end of the story? Why do you think he does this?   2 + 1
8 Look at the drawing on the right. Which Latin sentence best explains the old man's expression?   1

TOTAL   **10**

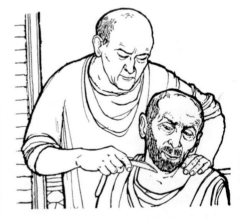

vēnālīcius

Caecilius ad portum ambulat. Caecilius portum circumspectat. argentārius nāvem Syriam videt, et ad nāvem ambulat. Syphāx prope nāvem stat.

'salvē, Syphāx!' clāmat argentārius. Syphāx est vēnālīcius. Syphāx Caecilium salūtat.

Caecilius servum quaerit. Syphāx rīdet. ecce! Syphāx magnum servum habet. Caecilius servum spectat. argentārius nōn est contentus. argentārius servum nōn emit.

'vīnum!' clāmat Syphāx. ancilla vīnum ad Caecilium portat. argentārius vīnum bibit.

Caecilius ancillam spectat. ancilla est pulchra. ancilla rīdet. ancilla Caecilium dēlectat. vēnālīcius quoque rīdet.

'Melissa cēnam optimam coquit', inquit vēnālīcius. 'Melissa linguam Latīnam discit. Melissa est docta et pulchra. Melissa ...'

'satis! satis!' clāmat Caecilius. Caecilius Melissam emit et ad vīllam revenit. Melissa Grumiōnem dēlectat. Melissa Quīntum dēlectat. ēheu! ancilla Metellam nōn dēlectat.

ad portum *to the harbour*
nāvem Syriam *Syrian ship*
prope nāvem *near the ship*

5

quaerit *is looking for*
habet *has*
contentus *satisfied*
emit *buys*

10

pulchra *beautiful*

linguam Latīnam *Latin language*
discit *is learning*
docta *skilful, educated*
satis *enough*
ēheu! *oh dear! oh no!*

15

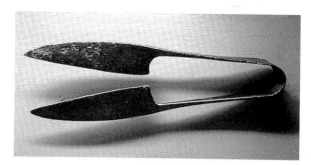

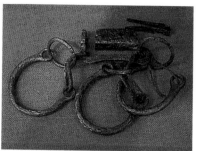

Tools of the trade. A pair of scissors; slave shackles with a padlock (not to same scale).

About the language

1   Remember the difference between the nominative case and
accusative case of the following nouns:

nominative	Metella	Caecilius	mercātor
accusative	Metellam	Caecilium	mercātōrem

2   A large number of words, such as **ancilla** and **taberna,** form
their accusative case in the same way as **Metella.** They are known
as the **first declension**, and look like this:

nominative	Metella	ancilla	taberna
accusative	Metellam	ancillam	tabernam

3   Another large group of nouns is known as the **second declension**.
Most of these words form their accusative in the same way as
Caecilius. For example:

nominative	Caecilius	servus	amīcus
accusative	Caecilium	servum	amīcum

4   You have also met several nouns belonging to the **third declension**.
For example:

nominative	mercātor	leō	senex
accusative	mercātōrem	leōnem	senem

The nominative ending of the third declension may take various forms,
but the accusative nearly always ends in **-em**.

*Pompeian householders loved to
have their walls painted with
pictures of gardens full of flowers
and birds, like this golden oriole.*

Practising the language

1   Write out each sentence, completing it with the right word from the brackets. Then translate the sentence.

    a   mercātor ē vīllā . . . . (quaerit, ambulat)
    b   servus ad hortum . . . . (recitat, venit)
    c   coquus ad culīnam . . . . (revenit, habet)
    d   Syphāx servum ad vīllam . . . . (dūcit, intrat)
    e   Clēmēns cibum ad Caecilium . . . . (clāmat, respondet, portat)

2   Write out each sentence, completing it with the right case of the noun from the brackets. Then translate the sentence.

    For example: . . . . vīnum portat.   (servus, servum)
                               servus vīnum portat.
                               The slave carries the wine.

    a   amīcus . . . . laudat. (servus, servum)
    b   senex . . . . intrat. (taberna, tabernam)
    c   . . . . cibum gustat. (dominus, dominum)
    d   . . . . Metellam salūtat. (mercātor, mercātōrem)
    e   vēnālīcius . . . . videt. (tōnsor, tōnsōrem)
    f   . . . . versum recitat. (poēta, poētam)
    g   . . . . in forō ambulat. (senex, senem)
    h   ancilla . . . . ad ātrium dūcit. (pictor, pictōrem)

The town of Pompeii

The town of Pompeii was built on a low hill of volcanic rock about eight kilometres (five miles) south of Mount Vesuvius and close to the mouth of a small river. It was one of a number of prosperous towns in the fertile region of Campania. Outside the towns, especially along the coast of the bay, there were many villas and farming estates, often owned by wealthy Romans who were attracted to the area by its pleasant climate and peaceful surroundings.

Villas along the bay.

The town itself covered 66 hectares (163 acres), and was surrounded by a wall. The wall had eleven towers and eight gates. Roads led out from these gates to the neighbouring towns of Herculaneum, Nola, Nuceria, Stabiae, and to the harbour.

Two wide main streets, known nowadays as the Street of Shops and Stabiae Street, crossed near the centre of the town. A third main street ran parallel to the Street of Shops. The other streets, most of which also ran in straight lines, divided the town neatly into blocks. Most streets probably did not have names, and a stranger visiting the town would have had to ask the way from the local people. The present names were invented in modern times to make it easier to identify the streets. The streets, constructed of volcanic stone, had high pavements on one or both sides to enable pedestrians to avoid the traffic of wagons, horses and mules, and to keep clear of the rubbish and rain water that collected in the roadway. Stepping-stones provided convenient crossing places.

A street in Pompeii in the rain.

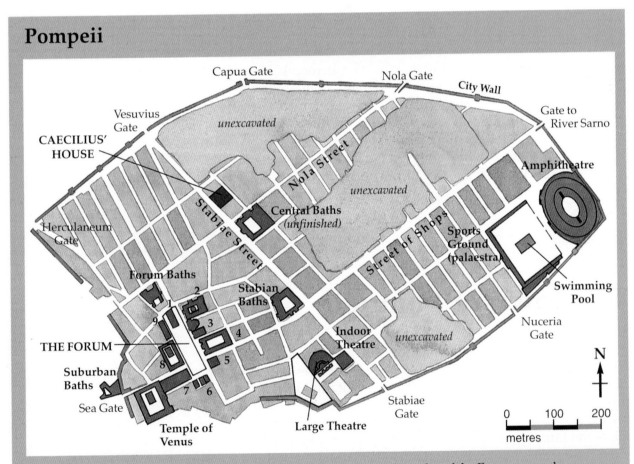

Pompeii

Buildings around the Forum: **1** Temple of Jupiter; **2** Market; **3** Temples of the Emperors and the Lares of Pompeii; **4** Eumachia's Clothworkers' Guildhall; **5** Polling station; **6** Municipal offices; **7** Basilica; **8** Temple of Apollo; **9** Vegetable market and public lavatory.

The town's water supply was brought from the hills by an aqueduct; on reaching Pompeii it was stored in large tanks on high ground at the northern side. The pressure created by the water in these tanks provided a good flow through underground lead pipes to all parts of the town, including the three sets of public baths. Public fountains, like this one in the Street of Shops, stood at many street corners. Most people drew their water from these, but wealthier citizens paid special rates so that they could take a private supply straight into their homes.

A bakery. On the left are two corn mills, worked by slaves or donkeys, and at the back is the bread oven.

In all the main streets there were bakers' shops and bars where hot and cold drinks and snacks could be bought. The main shopping areas were in the forum and along the Street of Shops to the north-east of the Stabian Baths. Carved or painted signs indicated different kinds of shop: the figure of a goat announced a dairy; a hammer and chisel advertised a stonemason. General advertisements and public notices were painted on the whitewashed walls outside shops and houses. We can still see notices advertising shows in the amphitheatre, and political slogans supporting candidates in the local elections.

At the western end of the town was the forum. This large and impressive open space, with a covered colonnade on three sides, was the centre for business, local government and religion.

Stabiae Street today.

The sign from a dairy.

There were two theatres. Popular shows for large audiences were performed in the big open-air theatre, which could hold about 5,000 people, while the smaller one, which was roofed, was used for concerts and for other shows. At the eastern end of the town was a huge sports ground or **palaestra**, and next to it an amphitheatre in which gladiatorial combats and wild-animal hunts were staged. This amphitheatre was large enough to seat every inhabitant in Pompeii and visitors from neighbouring towns as well.

Like a modern seaport, Pompeii was a place where people of many nationalities were to be seen: Romans, Greeks, Syrians, Jews, Africans, Spaniards and probably several other nationalities as well, with their different languages and different religions. This regular coming and going of people, many of whom were merchants and businessmen, was made possible by the peaceful conditions that existed throughout the provinces of the Roman empire at this time.

From Britain in the north-west to Syria and Palestine in the east, Rome maintained peace and provided firm government. The frontiers of the empire were held secure by Roman troops stationed at important points. A system of well-built roads made travel by land relatively easy and provided an effective means of communication between Rome and distant parts of the empire. For many purposes, particularly for trade, travel by sea was more convenient. Ships carried cargoes of building materials, foodstuffs and luxury goods across the Mediterranean; taxes were collected in the provinces and the wealth of Rome increased. Pompeii was not a large town, but played its part in the flourishing life of the empire.

A plaster cast of shop shutters.

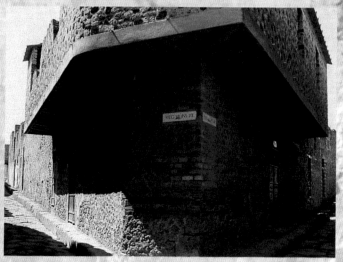

A house with its first storey overhanging the road to gain a little extra floor space; often the first floor was a separate flat. (The street signs are modern.)

A section of wall covered with painted slogans.

Counters, wine storage jars (amphorae) and serving jugs are still in place in some of the bars and food shops (left and right). Some also have paintings on the walls inside which show the customers drinking and gambling (above).

Vocabulary checklist 3

ad	*to*
bibit	*drinks*
circumspectat	*looks round*
clāmat	*shouts*
ecce!	*look!*
et	*and*
exit	*goes out*
exspectat	*waits for*
iānua	*door*
īrātus	*angry*
leō	*lion*
magnus	*big*
nāvis	*ship*
nōn	*not*
portat	*carries*
respondet	*replies*
rīdet	*laughs, smiles*
salvē!	*hello!*
surgit	*gets up, stands up*
taberna	*shop, inn*
videt	*sees*
vīnum	*wine*

This painting shows Mercury, the god of profit as well as the messenger of the gods. It is painted above a cloth workshop in the Street of Shops, to bring success to the business.

IN FORO

STAGE 4

1 Grumiō: ego sum coquus.
ego cēnam coquō.

2 Caecilius: ego sum argentārius.
ego pecūniam habeō.

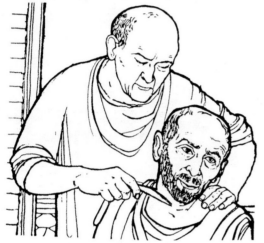

3 Pantagathus: ego sum tōnsor.
ego barbam tondeō.

4 Syphāx: ego sum vēnālīcius.
ego servum vēndō.

5 poēta: ego sum poēta.
ego versum recitō.

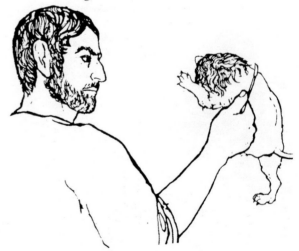

6 Celer: ego sum pictor.
ego leōnem pingō.

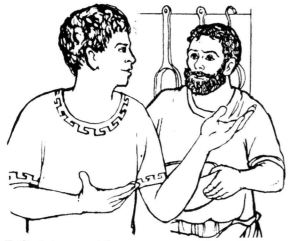

7 Quīntus: quid tū coquis?
  Grumiō: ego cēnam coquō.

8 Quīntus: quid tū habēs?
  Caecilius: ego pecūniam habeō.

9 Quīntus: quid tū tondēs?
  tōnsor: ego barbam tondeō.

10 Quīntus: quid tū vēndis?
   vēnālīcius: ego servum vēndō.

11 Quīntus: quid tū recitās?
   poēta: ego versum recitō.

12 Quīntus: quid tū pingis?
   pictor: ego leōnem pingō.

13 Metella: quis es tū?
ancilla: ego sum Melissa.

14 Metella: quis es tū?
vēnālīcius: ego sum Syphāx.

15 Metella: quis es tū?
servus: ego sum Clēmēns.

A corner of the forum, with shops opening off a colonnade.

Hermogenēs

Caecilius est in forō. Caecilius in forō argentāriam habet. Hermogenēs ad forum venit. Hermogenēs est mercātor Graecus. mercātor nāvem habet. mercātor Caecilium salūtat.

'ego sum mercātor Graecus', inquit Hermogenēs. 'ego sum mercātor probus. ego pecūniam quaerō.'

'cūr tū pecūniam quaeris?' inquit Caecilius. 'tū nāvem habēs.'

'sed nāvis nōn adest', respondet Hermogenēs. 'nāvis est in Graeciā. ego pecūniam nōn habeō. ego tamen sum probus. ego semper pecūniam reddō.'

'ecce!' inquit Caecilius. 'ego cēram habeō. tū ānulum habēs?'

'ego ānulum habeō', respondet Hermogenēs. 'ānulus signum habet. ecce! ego signum in cērā imprimō.'

Caecilius pecūniam trādit. mercātor pecūniam capit et ē forō currit.

ēheu! Hermogenēs nōn revenit. mercātor pecūniam nōn reddit. Caecilius Hermogenem ad basilicam vocat.

argentāriam *banker's stall*
Graecus *Greek*
probus *honest*
cūr? *why?*
nōn adest *is not here*
5 **in Graeciā** *in Greece*
tamen *however*
semper *always*
ego reddō *I give back*
cēram *wax tablet*
10 **ānulum** *ring*
signum *seal, sign*
ego imprimō *I press*
trādit *hands over*
capit *takes*
15 **currit** *runs*
ad basilicam *to the law court*

in basilicā

iūdex basilicam intrat.

iūdex:	quis es tū?
Caecilius:	ego sum Lūcius Caecilius Iūcundus.
iūdex:	tū es Pompēiānus?
Caecilius:	ego sum Pompēiānus.
iūdex:	quid tū in urbe agis?
Caecilius:	ego cotīdiē ad forum veniō. ego sum argentārius.
iūdex:	cūr tū hodiē ad basilicam venīs?
Caecilius:	Hermogenēs multam pecūniam dēbet. Hermogenēs pecūniam nōn reddit.
Hermogenēs:	Caecilius est mendāx!
iūdex:	quis es tū?
Hermogenēs:	ego sum Hermogenēs.
iūdex:	Hermogenēs, quid tū in urbe agis?
Hermogenēs:	ego in forō negōtium agō. ego sum mercātor.
iūdex:	quid tū respondēs? tū pecūniam dēbēs?
Hermogenēs:	ego pecūniam nōn dēbeō. amīcus meus est testis.
amīcus:	ego sum testis. Hermogenēs pecūniam nōn dēbet. Caecilius est mendāx.
Caecilius:	tū, Hermogenēs, es mendāx. amīcus tuus quoque est mendāx. tū pecūniam nōn reddis…
iūdex:	satis! tū Hermogenem accūsās, sed tū rem nōn probās.
Caecilius:	ego cēram habeō. tū signum in cērā vidēs.
Hermogenēs:	ēheu!
iūdex:	Hermogenēs, tū ānulum habēs?
Caecilius:	ecce! Hermogenēs ānulum cēlat.
iūdex:	ubi est ānulus? ecce! ānulus rem probat. ego Hermogenem convincō.

iūdex *judge*

quis? *who?*
Pompēiānus *a citizen of Pompeii*
5 **quid tū agis?** *what do you do?*
in urbe *in the city*
cotīdiē *every day*
hodiē *today*
dēbet *owes*

10

mendāx *liar*

15

meus *my, mine*
testis *witness*

20

tuus *your*

tū accūsās *you accuse*
25 **tū rem nōn probās** *you do not prove the case*

cēlat *is hiding*
ubi? *where?*
30 **ego convincō** *I convict, I find guilty*

Some seal-stones from rings and a gold seal-ring without a stone. The stone on the left is enlarged.

About the language

1   In the first three Stages, you met sentences like this:

ancilla ambulat.	mercātor sedet.	servus currit.
The slave-girl walks.	*The merchant sits.*	*The slave runs.*

All of these sentences have a noun (**ancilla, mercātor, servus**) and a word indicating the action of the sentence, known as the **verb**. In the sentences above the verbs are **ambulat, sedet, currit.**

In all the sentences you met in the first three Stages, the verb ended in **-t**.

2   In Stage 4, you have met sentences with **ego** and **tū**:

ego ambulō.	*I walk.*	**ego** sedeō.	*I sit.*	**ego** currō.	*I run.*
tū ambulās.	*You walk.*	**tū** sedēs.	*You sit.*	**tū** curris.	*You run.*

3   Notice the three different forms of each word:

ego ambulō.	ego sedeō.	ego currō.
tū ambulās.	tū sedēs.	tū curris.
ancilla ambulat.	mercātor sedet.	servus currit.

Notice also that the words **ego** and **tū** are not strictly necessary, since the endings **-ō** and **-s** make it clear that 'I' and 'you' are performing the action of the sentence. The Romans generally used **ego** and **tū** for emphasis.

4   The following example is rather different:

ego **sum** īrātus.	tū **es** īrātus.	servus **est** īrātus.
I am angry.	*You are angry.*	*The slave is angry.*

5   Further examples:

a Caecilius recitat. ego recitō.
b Quīntus dormit. tū dormīs.
c tū labōrās. servus labōrat.
d Syphāx servum habet. ego servum habeō.

e ego pecūniam trādō. tū pecūniam trādis.
f Pantagathus est tōnsor. tū es mercātor. ego sum poēta.
g ambulō; circumspectō; circumspectās; es.
h sum; audiō; audīs; habēs.

Practising the language

1   Write out each pair of sentences, completing the second sentence
    with the right verb from the brackets. Translate both sentences.

   a   ego sum coquus.
        ego cēnam . . . . (dormiō, coquō)
   b   ego sum mercātor.
        ego nāvem . . . . (stō, habeō)
   c   ego sum Herculēs.
        ego fūstem . . . . (teneō, sedeō)
   d   ego sum servus.
        ego in culīnā . . . . (habeō, labōrō)
   e   tū es amīcus.
        tū vīllam . . . . (intrās, dūcis)
   f   tū es ancilla.
        tū suāviter . . . . (venīs, cantās)
   g   tū es mendāx.
        tū pecūniam . . . . (dēbēs, ambulās)
   h   tū es iūdex.
        tū Hermogenem . . . . (curris, convincis)
   i   ego sum Syphāx.
        ego ancillam . . . . (vēndō, ambulō)
   j   tū es senex.
        tū in tabernā . . . . (tenēs, sedēs)

*The basilica (law court) was a
large, long building with rows of
pillars inside and a high platform
at one end on which the town's
senior officials sat when hearing
lawsuits. The platform is on the
left of the photograph.*

2 Translate this story:

Grumiō et leō

Celer in vīllā labōrat. Celer pictūram in triclīniō pingit.
magnus leō est in pictūrā. Celer ē vīllā discēdit.

Grumiō ē tabernā revenit et vīllam intrat. Grumiō est
ēbrius. Grumiō pictūram videt. Grumiō est perterritus.

'ēheu!' inquit Grumiō. 'leō est in triclīniō. leō mē   5
spectat. leō mē ferōciter petit.'

Grumiō ē triclīniō currit et culīnam intrat. Clēmēns
est in culīnā. Clēmēns Grumiōnem spectat.

'cūr tū es perterritus?' inquit Clēmēns.

'ēheu! leō est in triclīniō', inquit Grumiō.   10

'ita vērō', respondet Clēmēns, 'et servus ēbrius est in
culīnā.'

discēdit *departs, leaves*
ē tabernā *from the inn*
ēbrius *drunk*

ita vērō *yes*

*This comic painting comes from Pompeii
and shows a Roman-style trial taking
place before a judge and his two advisers,
with soldiers to keep order.*

*One of Caecilius' tablets, with a
special groove in the centre to
hold wax seals.*

The forum

The forum was the heart of the commercial, administrative and religious life of Pompeii. It was a large open space surrounded on three sides by a colonnade, with various important buildings grouped closely round it. The open area, 143 metres (156 yards) long and 38 metres (42 yards) wide, was paved with stone. In it stood a number of statues commemorating the emperor, members of the emperor's family, and local citizens who had given distinguished service to the town.

The drawing below shows a typical scene in the forum. The trader on the left has set up his wooden stall and is selling small articles of ironware, pincers, knives and hammers; the trader on the right is a shoemaker. He has seated his customers on stools while he shows them his goods. Behind the traders is the colonnade. This elegant structure, supported by columns of white marble, provided an open corridor in which people could walk and do business out of the heat of the sun in summer and out of the rain in winter.

In the same drawing are two statues of important citizens mounted on horseback. Behind them is one of the bronze gates through which people entered the forum. The whole forum area was for pedestrians only and a row of upright stones at each entrance provided an effective barrier to wheeled traffic. You can see two of these stones in the picture on page 39.

In the Pompeian wall-painting opposite, you see a public notice board fixed across the pedestals of three statues, and people studying the notices. There were no newspapers in Pompeii, but certain kinds of information, such as election results and dates of processions and shows, had to be publicised. This was done by putting up notice boards in the forum.

Part of the colonnade, which had two storeys, seen from inside. You can see the holes for the floor beams of the top storey.

Drawing based on a Pompeian wall-painting. Another scene from the same painting can be seen opposite.

In addition to official announcements, a large number of graffiti have been found in the forum and elsewhere, in which ordinary citizens recorded lost property, announced accommodation to let, left lovers' messages and publicised the problems they were having with their neighbours. One example reads:

> A bronze jar has been lost from this shop.
> A reward is offered for its recovery.

Another complains of noise at night and asks the **aedile** (the official who was responsible for law and order) to do something about it:

> Macerior requests the aedile to stop people from
> making a noise in the streets and disturbing
> decent folk who are asleep.

This statue of a distinguished citizen on horseback was found in nearby Herculaneum, but is very similar to the left-hand statue in the Pompeian painting above.

Some of the most important public buildings were situated round the forum. In a prominent position at the north end stood the temple of Jupiter, the greatest of the Roman gods (see 1 opposite). It was probably from the steps of this temple that political speeches were made at election times.

Next to the temple was a large covered market (2) which contained permanent shops rather than temporary stalls. The traders here sold mainly meat, fish and vegetables. A public weights and measures table (10) ensured that they gave fair measures.

Immediately to the south of the market was a temple dedicated to the **Larēs**, the guardian spirits of Pompeii (3), and next to that stood a temple in honour of the Roman Emperors (4). Across the forum was the temple of Apollo (9), and near the south-west corner of the forum was the temple of Venus, an important goddess for the Pompeians, who believed that she took a special interest in their town.

We have now mentioned five religious shrines around or near the forum. There were many others elsewhere in the town, including a temple of Isis, an Egyptian goddess, whose worship had been brought to Italy. In addition to these public shrines, each home had its own small shrine, the lararium, where the family's own lares, who looked after their household, were worshipped. The Pompeians believed in many gods, rather than one, and it seemed to them quite natural to believe that different gods should care for different parts of human life. Apollo, for example, was associated with law, medicine and music; Venus was the goddess of love and beauty.

On the east side of the forum (5) was the guildhall of the cloth trade (5), whose porch and colonnade were built with money given by Eumachia, a successful businesswoman and priestess. As this was one of the most prosperous industries in the town, it is not surprising that its headquarters were large and occupied such a prominent site.

Next to the guildhall was the polling station, an open hall used for voting in elections (6), and along the south side were three municipal offices (7), whose exact purpose is not known. They may have been the treasury, the record office and the meeting room of the town council.

At the south-west corner stood the **basilica**, or law court (8). The basilica was also used as a meeting place for businessmen.

Forum – focus of life

Business, religion, local government: these were the official purposes of the forum and its surrounding buildings. This great crowded square was the centre of much of the open-air life in Pompeii. Here people gathered to do business, to shop or to meet friends. Strangers visiting the forum would have been struck by its size, the splendid buildings surrounding it and the general air of prosperity.

Carving from Eumachia's Guildhall.

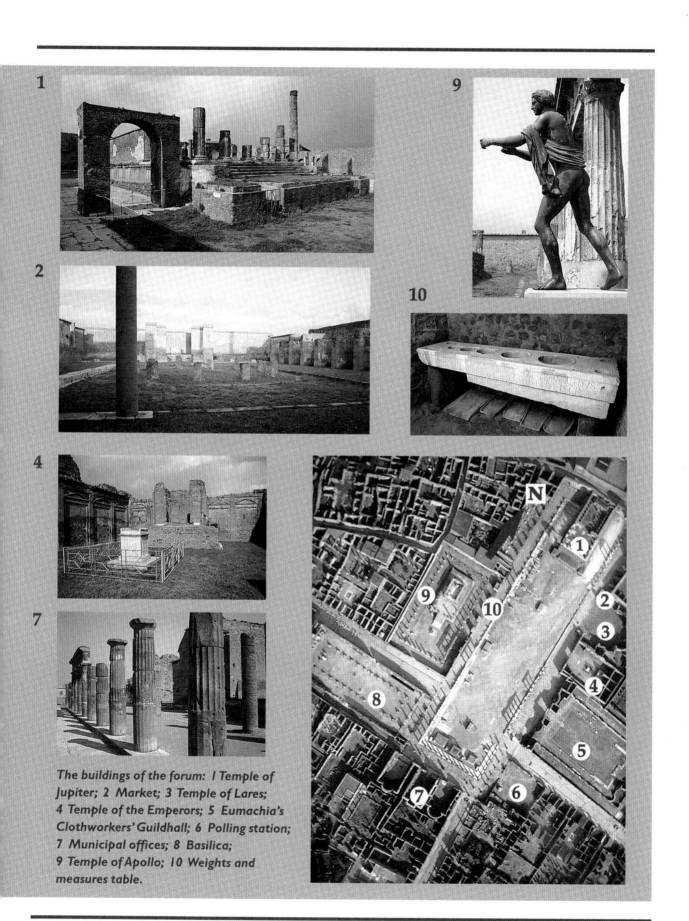

The buildings of the forum: 1 Temple of Jupiter; 2 Market; 3 Temple of Lares; 4 Temple of the Emperors; 5 Eumachia's Clothworkers' Guildhall; 6 Polling station; 7 Municipal offices; 8 Basilica; 9 Temple of Apollo; 10 Weights and measures table.

Vocabulary checklist 4

agit	does
ānulus	ring
coquit	cooks
cūr?	why?
ē	from, out of
ego	I
ēheu!	oh dear! oh no!
habet	has
inquit	says
iūdex	judge
mendāx	liar
pecūnia	money
perterritus	terrified
poēta	poet
quaerit	looks for, searches for
quis?	who?
reddit	gives back
satis	enough
sed	but
signum	sign, seal
tū	you
vocat	calls

This marble carving was found in Caecilius' house. It shows the temple of Jupiter with statues of men on horseback on each side, as it looked during an earthquake that happened in AD 62.

IN THEATRO

STAGE 5

in viā

1 canis est in viā.

2 canēs sunt in viā.

3 servus est in viā.

4 servī sunt in viā.

5 puella est in viā.

6 puellae sunt in viā.

7 puer est in viā.

8 puerī sunt in viā.

9 mercātor est in viā.

10 mercātōrēs sunt in viā.

in theātrō

11 spectātor in theātrō sedet.

12 spectātōrēs in theātrō sedent.

13 āctor in scaenā stat.

14 āctōrēs in scaenā stant.

15 fēmina spectat.

16 fēminae spectant.

17 senex dormit.

18 senēs dormiunt.

19 iuvenis plaudit.

20 iuvenēs plaudunt.

āctōrēs

magna turba est in urbe. fēminae et puellae sunt in turbā. senēs
quoque et iuvenēs sunt in turbā. servī hodiē nōn labōrant. senēs
hodiē nōn dormiunt. mercātōrēs hodiē nōn sunt occupātī.
· Pompēiānī sunt ōtiōsī. urbs tamen nōn est quiēta. Pompēiānī ad
theātrum contendunt. magnus clāmor est in urbe.
    agricolae urbem intrant. nautae urbem petunt. pāstōrēs dē
· monte veniunt et ad urbem contendunt. turba per portam ruit.
    nūntius in forō clāmat: 'āctōrēs sunt in urbe. āctōrēs sunt in
theātrō. Priscus fābulam dat. Priscus fābulam optimam dat.
āctōrēs sunt Actius et Sorex.'
    Caecilius et Metella ē vīllā discēdunt. argentārius et uxor ad
theātrum ambulant. Clēmēns et Melissa ad theātrum
contendunt. sed Grumiō in vīllā manet.

āctōrēs	*actors*

turba *crowd*
fēminae *women*
puellae *girls*
iuvenēs *young men*
5 **ōtiōsī** *on holiday, idle*
quiēta *quiet*
ad theātrum *to the theatre*
contendunt *hurry*
clāmor *shout, uproar*
10 **agricolae** *farmers*
nautae *sailors*
petunt *make for, seek*
pāstōrēs *shepherds*
dē monte *down from the mountain*
per portam ruit *rushes through the gate*
nūntius *messenger*
fābulam dat *is putting on a play*
uxor *wife*
manet *remains, stays*

Two actors in mask and costume. These statues were found in the garden of a house in Pompeii.

About the language 1

1   In the first four Stages, you have met sentences like these:

            puella sedet.   servus labōrat.
            The girl is sitting.   *The slave is working.*

            leō currit.   mercātor dormit.
            The lion is running.   *The merchant is sleeping.*

   Sentences like these refer to **one** person or thing, and in each sentence the form of both words (the noun and the verb) is said to be **singular.**

2   Sentences which refer to **more than one** person or thing use a different form of the words, known as the **plural.** Compare the singular and plural forms in the following sentences:

       singular   *plural*
       puella labōrat.   puellae labōrant.
       The girl is working.   *The girls are working.*

       servus rīdet.   servī rīdent.
       The slave is laughing.   *The slaves are laughing.*

       leō currit.   leōnēs currunt.
       The lion is running.   *The lions are running.*

       mercātor dormit.   mercātōrēs dormiunt.
       The merchant is sleeping.   *The merchants are sleeping.*

   Note that in each of these sentences **both** the noun and the verb show the difference between singular and plural.

3   Look again at the sentences in paragraph 2 and note the difference between the singular and plural forms of the verb.

       singular   *plural*
       labōrat   labōrant
       rīdet   rīdent
       currit   currunt
       dormit   dormiunt

   In each case the singular ending is **-t** and the plural ending is **-nt**.

4   Notice how Latin shows the difference between 'is' and 'are':

mercātor **est** in viā.   mercātōrēs **sunt** in viā.
The merchant is in the street.   *The merchants are in the street.*

*Fragment of wall-painting
showing an actor in the dressing-room,
studying his mask.*

Poppaea

Poppaea est ancilla. ancilla prope iānuam stat. ancilla viam spectat.
dominus in hortō dormit. dominus est Lucriō. Lucriō est senex.

Poppaea:	ego amīcum meum exspectō. ubi est amīcus?
	(Lucriō stertit.)
	ēheu! Lucriō est in vīllā.
	(agricolae in viā clāmant.)
agricolae:	euge! agricolae hodiē nōn labōrant!
Poppaea:	Lucriō! Lucriō! agricolae urbem intrant.
	agricolae adsunt.
Lucriō:	*(sēmisomnus)* a…a…agricolae?
puerī:	euge! Sorex! Actius! āctōrēs adsunt.
Poppaea:	Lucriō! Lucriō! puerī per viam currunt.
Lucriō:	quid tū clāmās, Poppaea? cūr tū clāmōrem facis?
Poppaea:	Lucriō, Pompēiānī clāmōrem faciunt.
	agricolae et puerī sunt in viā.
Lucriō:	cūr tū mē vexās?
Poppaea:	āctōrēs in theātrō fābulam agunt.
Lucriō:	āctōrēs?
Poppaea:	Sorex et Actius adsunt.
Lucriō:	quid tū dīcis?
Poppaea:	*(īrāta)* senēs ad theātrum ambulant, iuvenēs
	ad theātrum contendunt, omnēs Pompēiānī
	ad theātrum ruunt. āctōrēs in theātrō fābulam agunt.
Lucriō:	euge! āctōrēs adsunt. ego quoque ad theātrum
	contendō.
	(exit Lucriō. amīcus vīllam intrat.)
amīcus:	salvē! mea columba!
Poppaea:	Grumiō, dēliciae meae! salvē!
Grumiō:	ubi est dominus tuus?
Poppaea:	Lucriō abest.
Grumiō:	euge!

euge! *hurray!*

5

adsunt *are here*
sēmisomnus *half-asleep*

10

puerī *boys*
tū clāmōrem facis *you are*
                making a noise

15

tū vexās *you annoy*
fābulam agunt *act a play*

20

tū dīcis *you say*

omnēs *all*
ruunt *rush*

25

mea columba *my dove, my dear*
dēliciae meae *my darling*

30

abest *is out*

About the language 2

1 Study the following examples of singular and plural forms:

singular	plural
puella rīdet.	**puellae** rīdent.
The girl is smiling.	The girls are smiling.
servus ambulat.	**servī** ambulant.
The slave is walking.	The slaves are walking.
mercātor contendit.	**mercātōrēs** contendunt.
The merchant is hurrying.	The merchants are hurrying.

2 Each of the nouns in **bold type** is in the nominative case, because it refers to a person or persons who are performing some action, such as walking or smiling.

3 **puella**, **servus** and **mercātor** are therefore **nominative singular**, and **puellae, servī** and **mercātōrēs** are **nominative plural**.

4 Notice the forms of the nominative plural in the different declensions:

first declension	second declension	third declension
puellae	servī	mercātōrēs
ancillae	amīcī	leōnēs
fēminae	puerī	senēs

5 Further examples:

a amīcus ambulat. amīcī ambulant.
b āctor clāmat. āctōrēs clāmant.
c fēminae plaudunt. fēmina plaudit.
d vēnālīciī intrant. vēnālīcius intrat.
e ancilla respondet. ancillae respondent.
f senēs dormiunt. senex dormit.

Practising the language

1   Write out each sentence, completing it with the right form of the verb from the brackets. Then translate the sentence.

> For example: senēs . . . . (dormit, dormiunt)
> senēs **dormiunt**.
> *The old men are sleeping.*

   a āctōrēs . . . . (adest, adsunt)
   b puellae in theātrō . . . . (sedent, sedet)
   c agricolae ad urbem . . . . (currunt, currit)
   d Pompēiānī clāmōrem . . . . (facit, faciunt)
   e servī ad theātrum . . . . (contendit, contendunt)

2   Write out each sentence, completing it with the right form of the verb from the brackets. Then translate the sentence.

   a pāstōrēs ad theātrum . . . . (contendit, contendunt)
   b pāstor pecūniam nōn . . . . (habet, habent)
   c puella āctōrem . . . . (laudat, laudant)
   d fēminae fābulam . . . . (spectat, spectant)
   e vēnālīciī ad urbem . . . . (venit, veniunt)
   f nūntius in forō . . . . (clāmat, clāmant)
   g senēs in forō . . . . (dormit, dormiunt)
   h pater . . . . in tablīnō. (est, sunt)

3   Translate this story:

in theātrō

hodiē Pompēiānī sunt ōtiōsī. dominī et servī nōn
labōrant. multī Pompēiānī in theātrō sedent.
spectātōrēs Actium exspectant. tandem Actius in
scaenā stat. Pompēiānī plaudunt.
   subitō Pompēiānī magnum clāmōrem audiunt.   5
servus theātrum intrat. 'euge! fūnambulus adest',
clāmat servus. Pompēiānī Actium nōn spectant. omnēs
Pompēiānī ē theātrō currunt et fūnambulum spectant.
   nēmō in theātrō manet. Actius tamen nōn est īrātus.
Actius quoque fūnambulum spectat.

multī	*many*
spectātōrēs	*spectators*
tandem	*at last*
in scaenā	*on the stage*
plaudunt	*applaud, clap*
subitō	*suddenly*
fūnambulus	*tight-rope walker*
nēmō	*no one*

The theatre at Pompeii

Plays were not performed in Pompeii every day but only at festivals, which were held several times a year. There was therefore all the more excitement in the town when the notices appeared announcing a performance. On the day itself the shops were closed and no business was done in the forum. Men and women with their slaves set off for the theatre early in the morning. Some carried cushions, because the seats were made of stone, and many took food and drink for the day. The only people who did not need to hurry were the town councillors and other important citizens, for whom the best seats at the front of the auditorium were reserved. These important people carried tokens which indicated the entrance they should use and where they were to sit. Late-comers among the ordinary citizens had to be content with a seat right at the top of the large semicircular auditorium. The large theatre at Pompeii could hold 5,000 people.

A dramatic performance was a public occasion, and admission to the theatre was free. All the expenses were paid by a wealthy citizen, who provided the actors, the producer, the scenery and costumes. He volunteered to do this, not only to benefit his fellow-citizens, but also to gain popularity which would be useful in local political elections.

A bronze head of Sorex, a famous Pompeian actor. Originally the eyes would have been inserted in life-like colours.

Pompeii's smaller, roofed theatre.

Pompeii's main, open-air theatre.

The performance consisted of a series of plays and lasted all day, even during the heat of the afternoon. To keep the spectators cool, a large awning was suspended by ropes and pulleys across most of the theatre. The awning was managed by sailors, who were used to handling ropes and canvas; even so, on a windy day the awning could not be unfurled, and the audience had to make use of hats or sunshades to protect themselves from the sun. Between plays, scented water was sprinkled by attendants.

One of the most popular kinds of production was the **pantomime**, a mixture of opera and ballet. The plot, which was usually serious, was taken from the Greek myths. The parts of the different characters were mimed and danced by one masked performer, while a chorus sang the lyrics. An orchestra containing such instruments as the lyre, double pipes, trumpet and castanets accompanied the performance, providing a rhythmical beat. Pantomime actors were usually Greek slaves or freedmen. They were much admired for their skill and stamina, and attracted a large following of fans.

Equally popular were the comic actors. The bronze statue of one of these, Sorex, was discovered at Pompeii, together with graffiti on walls naming other popular actors. One of these reads:

Actius, our favourite, come back quickly

A mosaic of a theatre musician.

A clay model of a mask, perhaps for the character Manducus.

The comedies of Plautus

There is usually a young man from a respectable family who is leading a wild life; he is often in debt and in love with a pretty but unsuitable slave-girl. His father, who is old-fashioned and disapproving, has to be kept in the dark by deception. The son is usually helped in this by a cunning slave, who gets himself and his young master in and out of trouble at great speed. Eventually it is discovered that the girl is free-born and from a good family. The young man is therefore able to marry his true love and all ends happily.

Comic actors appeared in vulgar farces and in short one-act plays which were often put on at the end of longer performances. These short plays were about Italian country life and were packed with rude jokes and slapstick. They used just a few familiar characters, such as Pappus, an old fool, and Manducus, a greedy clown. These characters were instantly recognisable from the strange masks worn by the actors. The Roman poet, Juvenal, describes a performance of a play of this kind in a country theatre, where the children sitting on their mothers' laps shrank back in horror when they saw the gaping, white masks. These masks, like those used in other plays, were probably made of linen which was covered with plaster and painted.

Sometimes, at a festival, the comedies of Plautus and Terence may have been put on. These plays also used a number of familiar characters, but the plots were complicated and the dialogue more witty than that of the farces.

1 Father has to be restrained from violence when
   he finds his son coming home drunk from a party.
   The cunning slave props the lad up. A musician
   is playing the double pipes.

2 The boy has been with his
   beloved slave-girl (here's her
   mask).

3 The slave sits on an altar for sanctuary,
   hoping to escape terrible punishment.

4 The slave uncovers a basket in the girl's
   possession and finds her baby clothes –
   they are recognised! She must be the
   long-lost daughter of father's best friend
   and wrongly enslaved by pirates! All live
   happily ever after.

Vocabulary checklist 5

adest	*is here*
adsunt	*are here*
agricola	*farmer*
ambulat	*walks*
audit	*hears*
clāmor	*shout, uproar*
contendit	*hurries*
currit	*runs*
fābula	*play, story*
fēmina	*woman*
hodiē	*today*
iuvenis	*young man*
meus	*my, mine*
multus	*much*
multī	*many*
optimus	*very good, excellent*
petit	*makes for, attacks*
plaudit	*applauds*
puella	*girl*
senex	*old man*
spectat	*looks at, watches*
stat	*stands*
turba	*crowd*
ubi?	*where?*
urbs	*city*
venit	*comes*

This tight-rope walker from a wall-painting is a satyr, one of the followers of Bacchus, god of wine. He has a tail and plays the double pipes.

FELIX

STAGE 6

1 servī per viam ambulābant.

2 canis subitō lātrāvit.

3 Grumiō canem timēbat.

4 'pestis!' clāmāvit coquus.

5 Clēmēns erat fortis.

6 sed canis Clēmentem superāvit.

7 Quīntus per viam ambulābat.

8 iuvenis clāmōrem audīvit.

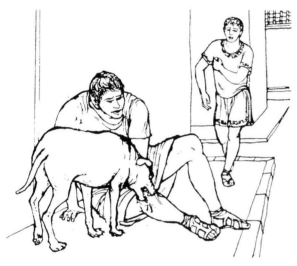

9 canis Clēmentem vexābat.

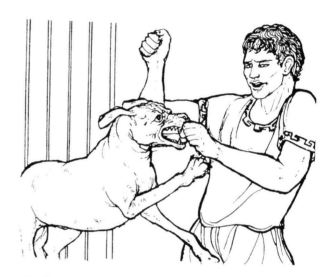

10 Quīntus canem pulsāvit.

11 servī erant laetī.

12 servī Quīntum laudāvērunt.

pugna

Clēmēns in forō ambulābat. turba maxima erat in forō. servī et
ancillae cibum emēbant. multī pistōrēs pānem vēndēbant. poēta
recitābat. mercātor Graecus contentiōnem cum agricolā habēbat.
mercātor īrātus pecūniam postulābat. subitō agricola Graecum
pulsāvit, quod Graecus agricolam vituperābat. Pompēiānī
rīdēbant, et agricolam incitābant. Clēmēns, postquam clāmōrem
audīvit, ad pugnam festīnāvit. tandem agricola mercātōrem
superāvit et ē forō agitāvit. Pompēiānī agricolam fortem
laudāvērunt.

pugna *fight*

maxima *very large*
erat *was*
pistōrēs *bakers*
pānem vēndēbant *were selling bread*
contentiōnem habēbat *was having an argument*
cum agricolā *with a farmer*
postulābat *was demanding*
pulsāvit *hit, punched*
quod *because*
incitābant *were urging on*
postquam *when, after*
festīnāvit *hurried*
superāvit *overpowered*
agitāvit *chased*

Fēlīx

multī Pompēiānī in tabernā vīnum bibēbant. Clēmēns tabernam
intrāvit. subitō Clēmēns 'Fēlīx!' clāmāvit. Clēmēns Fēlīcem laetē
salūtāvit. Fēlīx erat lībertus.
   Clēmēns Fēlīcem ad vīllam invītāvit. Clēmēns et Fēlīx vīllam
intrāvērunt. Clēmēns Caecilium et Metellam quaesīvit. Caecilius
in tablīnō scrībēbat. Metella in hortō sedēbat. Caecilius et
Metella ad ātrium festīnāvērunt et Fēlīcem salūtāvērunt.
postquam Quīntus ātrium intrāvit, Fēlīx iuvenem spectāvit.
lībertus erat valdē commōtus. paene lacrimābat; sed rīdēbat.
   tum Clēmēns ad culīnam festīnāvit. Grumiō in culīnā
dormiēbat. Clēmēns coquum excitāvit et tōtam rem nārrāvit.
coquus, quod erat laetus, cēnam optimam parāvit.

laetē *happily*
lībertus *freedman, ex-slave*
invītāvit *invited*

valdē commōtus *very moved, very much affected*
paene lacrimābat *was almost crying, was almost in tears*
tum *then*
excitāvit *aroused, woke up*
tōtam rem *the whole story*
nārrāvit *told*
parāvit *prepared*

Fēlīx et fūr

Felix

post cēnam Quīntus rogāvit, 'pater, cūr Fēlīx nunc est lībertus? ōlim erat servus tuus.'

   tum pater tōtam rem nārrāvit.

Caecilius:	Fēlīx ōlim in tablīnō scrībēbat. Fēlīx erat sōlus. Clēmēns et Grumiō cibum in forō quaerēbant. Metella aberat, quod sorōrem vīsitābat.
Fēlīx:	pater tuus aberat, quod argentāriam in forō administrābat.
Caecilius:	nēmō erat in vīllā nisi Fēlīx et īnfāns. parvus īnfāns in cubiculō dormiēbat. subitō fūr per iānuam intrāvit. fūr tacitē ātrium circumspectāvit; tacitē cubiculum intrāvit, ubi īnfāns erat. Fēlīx nihil audīvit, quod intentē labōrābat. fūr parvum īnfantem ē vīllā tacitē portābat. subitō īnfāns vāgīvit. Fēlīx, postquam clāmōrem audīvit, statim ē tablīnō festīnāvit.
	'furcifer!' clāmāvit Fēlīx īrātus, et fūrem ferōciter pulsāvit. Fēlīx fūrem paene necāvit. ita Fēlīx parvum īnfantem servāvit.
Fēlīx:	dominus, postquam rem audīvit, erat laetus et mē līberāvit. ego igitur sum lībertus.
Quīntus:	sed quis erat īnfāns?
Caecilius:	erat Quīntus!

fūr thief

post after
rogāvit asked
nunc now
ōlim once, some time ago
sōlus alone
5

aberat was out
sorōrem sister
administrābat was looking after
nisi except
10 *īnfāns* child, baby
parvus little
in cubiculō in a bedroom
tacitē quietly
ubi where
15 *nihil* nothing
portābat began to carry
vāgīvit cried, wailed
statim at once
necāvit killed
20 *ita* in this way
servāvit saved
līberāvit freed, set free
igitur therefore, and so

About the language

1   All the stories in the first five Stages were set in the present, and
    in every sentence the verbs were in the **present tense**. Study the
    following examples:

PRESENT TENSE

singular   servus **labōrat.**   *The slave works* or *The slave is working.*
plural   servī **labōrant.**   *The slaves work* or *The slaves are working.*

2   In Stage 6, because the stories happened in the past, you have
    met the **imperfect tense** and the **perfect tense**. Study the different
    endings of the two past tenses and their English translation:

IMPERFECT TENSE

singular   poēta **recitābat.**   *A poet was reciting.*
             Metella in hortō **sedēbat.**   *Metella was sitting in the garden.*

plural   servī in forō **ambulābant.**   *The slaves were walking in the forum.*
             Pompēiānī vīnum **bibēbant.**   *The Pompeians were drinking wine.*

PERFECT TENSE

singular   coquus **intrāvit.**   *The cook entered.*
             Clēmēns clāmōrem **audīvit.**   *Clemens heard the uproar.*

plural   amīcī Caecilium **salūtāvērunt.** *The friends greeted Caecilius.*
             iuvenēs ad tabernam **festīnāvērunt.** *The young men hurried to an inn.*

3   Compare the endings of the imperfect and perfect tenses with the
    endings of the present tense.

	singular	*plural*
PRESENT	portat	portant
IMPERFECT	portābat	portābant
PERFECT	portāvit	portāvērunt

You can see that in the imperfect and perfect tenses, as with the
present tense, the singular ends in **-t** and the plural in **-nt**.

4 Notice how Latin shows the difference between 'is', 'are'
   and 'was', 'were'.

	singular	*plural*
PRESENT	Caecilius **est** in tablīnō.	servī **sunt** in culīnā.
	Caecilius is in the study.	*The slaves are in the kitchen.*
IMPERFECT	Caecilius **erat** in forō.	servī **erant** in viā.
	Caecilius was in the forum.	*The slaves were in the street.*

5 In the following examples you will see that the imperfect
   tense is often used of an action or situation which was going
   on for some time.

   īnfāns in cubiculō **dormiēbat.**   pater et māter **aberant.**
   The baby was sleeping in the bedroom.   *The father and mother were away.*

6 The perfect tense, on the other hand, is often used of a completed
   action or an action that happened once.

   agricola mercātōrem **pulsāvit.**   Pompēiānī agricolam **laudāvērunt.**
   The farmer punched the merchant.   *The Pompeians praised the farmer.*

*This well-preserved bar at
Herculaneum gives us a good
impression of the taberna where
Clemens met Felix.*

Practising the language

1 When you have read the following story, answer the questions at the end.

avārus

duo fūrēs ōlim ad vīllam contendēbant. in vīllā mercātor
habitābat. mercātor erat senex et avārus. avārus multam
pecūniam habēbat. fūrēs, postquam vīllam intrāvērunt,
ātrium circumspectāvērunt.
  'avārus', inquit fūr, 'est sōlus. avārus servum nōn habet.' 5
  tum fūrēs tablīnum intrāvērunt. avārus clāmāvit et
ferōciter pugnāvit, sed fūrēs senem facile superāvērunt.
  'ubi est pecūnia, senex?' rogāvit fūr.
  'servus fidēlis pecūniam in cubiculō custōdit', inquit senex.
  'tū servum fidēlem nōn habēs, quod avārus es', clāmāvit 10
fūr. tum fūrēs cubiculum petīvērunt.
  'pecūniam videō', inquit fūr. fūrēs cubiculum intrāvērunt,
ubi pecūnia erat, et pecūniam intentē spectāvērunt. sed ēheu!
ingēns serpēns in pecūniā iacēbat. fūrēs serpentem timēbant
et ē vīllā celeriter festīnāvērunt. 15
  in vīllā avārus rīdēbat et serpentem laudābat.
  'tū es optimus servus. numquam dormīs. pecūniam
meam semper servās.'

avārus *miser*

duo *two*
habitābat *was living*

inquit *said*

pugnāvit *fought*
facile *easily*
fidēlis *faithful*
custōdit *is guarding*

ingēns *huge*
serpēns *snake*
iacēbat *was lying*
timēbant *were afraid of,*
        feared
celeriter *quickly*
numquam *never*
servās *look after*

ingēns serpēns.

Questions

		Marks
1	Who was hurrying to the merchant's house?	1
2	In lines 2 and 3, there is a description of the merchant. Write down three details about him.	3
3	What did the thieves do immediately after entering the house?	1
4	In line 5, why did one of the thieves think the merchant would be alone?	1
5	In line 7, which two Latin words tell you that the merchant resisted the thieves? Why did he lose the fight?	2 + 1
6	In line 9, who did the merchant say was guarding his money? Why did the thief think he was lying?	1 + 2
7	Which room did the thieves then enter? What did they see there?	1 + 2
8	Why did the thieves run away, lines 14–15?	1
9	In lines 17–18, how did the merchant describe the **serpēns**? What reasons did he give?	1 + 2
10	In line 6, the thieves found the merchant in his study. What do you think he was doing there?	1

TOTAL **20**

---

2 Write out each sentence completing it with the right form of the noun from the brackets. Then translate the Latin sentence. Take care with the meaning of the tenses of the verb.

For example: . . . . in forō ambulābat. (servus, servī)
servus in forō ambulābat.
The slave was walking in the forum.

. . . . forum intrāvērunt. (amīcus, amīcī)
amīcī forum intrāvērunt.
The friends entered the forum.

a . . . . per viam festīnābat. (lībertus, lībertī)
b . . . . pecūniam portābant. (servus, servī)
c . . . . ātrium circumspectāvit. (fūr, fūrēs)
d . . . . clāmōrem audīvērunt. (mercātor, mercātōrēs)
e . . . . fūrem superāvērunt. (puer, puerī)
f . . . . ad urbem festīnāvit. (nauta, nautae)

Slaves and freedmen

Wherever you travelled in the Roman world, you would find people who were slaves, like Grumio, Clemens and Melissa. They belonged to a master or mistress, to whom they had to give complete obedience; they were not free to make decisions for themselves; they could not marry; nor could they own personal possessions or be protected by courts of law. The law, in fact, did not regard them as human beings, but as things that could be bought and sold, treated well or treated badly, according to the whim of their master. These people carried out much of the hard manual work but they also took part in many skilled trades and occupations. They did not live separately from free people; many slaves would live in the same house as their master, usually occupying rooms in the rear part of the house. Slaves and free people could often be found working together.

The Romans and others who lived around the Mediterranean in classical times regarded slavery as a normal and necessary part of life. Even those who realised that it was not a natural state of affairs made no serious attempt to abolish it.

People usually became slaves as a result either of being taken prisoner in war or of being captured by pirates; the children of slaves were automatically born into slavery. They came from many different tribes and countries, Gaul and Britain, Spain and North Africa, Egypt, different parts of Greece and Asia Minor, Syria and Palestine. By the time of the Emperor Augustus at the beginning of the first century AD, there were perhaps as many as three slaves for every five free citizens in Italy. Most families owned at least one or two; a merchant like Caecilius would have no fewer than a dozen in his house and many more working on his estates and in his businesses. Very wealthy men owned

Many people became slaves when captured in Rome's numerous wars. The scene on the left shows captives after a battle, sitting among the captured weapons and waiting to be sold. Families would be split up and slaves would be given new names by their masters.

hundreds and sometimes even thousands of slaves. A man called Pedanius Secundus, who lived in Rome, kept four hundred in his house there; when one of them murdered him, they were all put to death, in spite of protests by the people of Rome.

The work and treatment of slaves

Slaves were employed in all kinds of work. In the country, their life was rougher and harsher than in the cities. They worked as labourers on farms, as shepherds and cowherds on the big estates in southern Italy, in the mines and on the building of roads and bridges. Some of the strongest slaves were bought for training as gladiators.

In the towns, slaves were used for both unskilled and skilled work. They were cooks and gardeners, general servants, labourers in factories, secretaries, musicians, actors and entertainers. In the course of doing such jobs, they were regularly in touch with their masters and other free men; they moved without restriction about the streets of the towns, went shopping, visited temples and were also quite often present in the theatre and at shows in the amphitheatre. Foreign visitors to Rome and Italy were sometimes surprised that there was so little visible difference between a slave and a poor free man.

Some masters were cruel and brutal to their slaves, but others were kind and humane. Common sense usually prevented a master from treating his slaves too harshly, since only fit, well-cared-for slaves were likely to work efficiently. A slave who was a skilled craftsman, particularly one who was able to read and write, keep accounts and manage the work of a small shop, would have cost a large sum of money; and a Roman master was generally too sensible to waste an expensive possession through carelessness.

Slaves' jobs varied from serving drinks in the home and nursing children, to heavy labour, such as portering.

Some were trained as gladiators.

Freeing a slave

Not all slaves remained in slavery until they died. Freedom was sometimes given as a reward for particularly good service, sometimes as a sign of friendship and respect. Freedom was also very commonly given after the owner's death by a statement in the will. But the law laid down certain limits. For example, a slave could not be freed before he was thirty years old; and not more than a hundred slaves (fewer in a small household) could be freed in a will.

Masters were free to beat unsatisfactory slaves. House slaves were often punished by being sent to work on the owner's farm.

The act of freeing a slave was called **manūmissiō**. This word is connected with two other words, **manus** (hand) and **mittō** (send), and means 'a sending out from the hand' or 'setting free from control'. Manumission was performed in several ways. The oldest method took the form of a legal ceremony before a public official, such as a judge. This is the ceremony seen in the picture at the beginning of this Stage. A witness claimed that the slave did not really belong to the master at all; the master did not deny the claim; the slave's head was then touched with a rod and he was declared officially free. There were other, simpler methods. A master might manumit a slave by making a declaration in the presence of friends at home or merely by an invitation to recline on the couch at dinner.

Freedmen

The ex-slave became a **lībertus** (freedman). He now had the opportunity to make his own way in life, and possibly to become an important member of his community. He did not, however, receive all the privileges of a citizen who had been born free. He could not stand as a candidate in public elections, nor could he become a high-ranking officer in the army. He still had obligations to his former master and had to work for him a fixed number of days each year. He would become one of his clients and would visit him regularly to pay his respects, usually early in the morning. He would be expected to help and support his former master whenever he could. This connection between them is seen very clearly in the names taken by a freedman. Suppose that his slave-name had been Felix and his master had been Lucius Caecilius Iucundus. As soon as he was freed, Felix would take some of the names of his former master and call himself Lucius Caecilius Felix.

Some freedmen continued to do the same work that they had previously done as slaves; others were set up in business by their former masters. Others became priests in the temples or servants of the town council; the council secretaries, messengers, town clerk and town crier were all probably freedmen. Some became very rich and powerful. Two freedmen at Pompeii, who were called the Vettii and were possibly brothers, owned a house which is one of the most magnificent in the town. The colourful paintings on its walls and the elegant marble fountains in the garden show clearly how prosperous the Vettii were. Another Pompeian freedman was the architect who designed the large theatre; another was the father of Lucius Caecilius Iucundus.

A female ex-slave was called a **līberta** and had fewer opportunities than a freedman. Often a freedwoman would marry her former master.

The peristylium of the House of the Vettii.

Vocabulary checklist 6

abest	is out, is absent
aberat	was out, was absent
cubiculum	bedroom
emit	buys
ferōciter	fiercely
festīnat	hurries
fortis	brave
fūr	thief
intentē	intently, carefully
lībertus	freedman, ex-slave
ōlim	once, some time ago
parvus	small
per	through
postquam	after
pulsat	hits, thumps
quod	because
rēs	thing
scrībit	writes
subitō	suddenly
superat	overcomes, overpowers
tum	then
tuus	your, yours
vēndit	sells
vituperat	blames, curses

The two freedmen called the Vettii had their best dining-room decorated with tiny pictures of cupids, seen here racing in chariots drawn by deer.

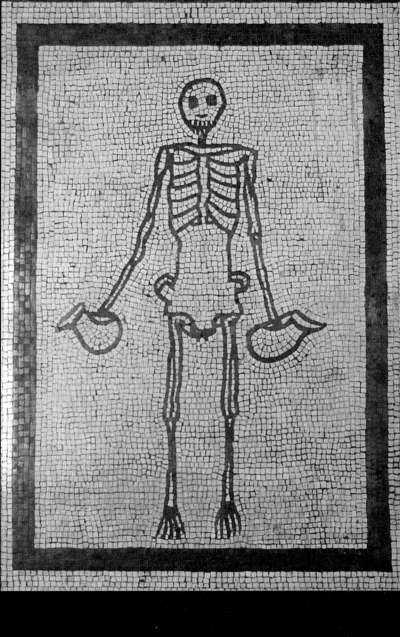

CENA

1 amīcus Caecilium vīsitābat. vīllam intrāvit.

2 Caecilius amīcum exspectābat. amīcum salūtāvit.

3 amīcus cum Caeciliō cēnābat. cēnam laudāvit.

4 amīcus pōculum īnspexit. vīnum gustāvit.

5 amīcus pōculum hausit. tum fābulam longam nārrāvit.

6 Caecilius plausit. 'euge!' dīxit.

7 amīcī optimum vīnum bibērunt. tandem
surrēxērunt.

8 servī in ātriō stābant. iānuam aperuērunt.

9 amīcus 'valē' dīxit. ē vīllā discessit.

fābula mīrābilis

multī amīcī cum Caeciliō cēnābant. Fēlīx quoque aderat. omnēs amīcī coquum laudāvērunt, quod cēna erat optima.

postquam omnēs cēnāvērunt, Caecilius clāmāvit, 'ubi est Decēns? Decēns nōn adest.' tum Caecilius Clēmentem ē vīllā mīsit. servus Decentem per urbem quaesīvit.

postquam servus ē vīllā discessit, Fēlīx pōculum hausit. tum lībertus fābulam mīrābilem nārrāvit:

'ōlim amīcus meus ex urbe discēdēbat. nox erat, sed lūna plēna lūcēbat. amīcus per viam festīnābat, ubi silva erat, et subitō centuriōnem cōnspexit. amīcus meus centuriōnem salūtāvit. centuriō tamen nihil dīxit. tum centuriō tunicam dēposuit. ecce! centuriō ēvānuit. ingēns lupus subitō appāruit. amīcus meus valdē timēbat. ingēns lupus ululāvit et ad silvam festīnāvit. tunica in viā iacēbat. amīcus tunicam cautē īnspexit. ecce! tunica erat lapidea. tum amīcus rem intellēxit. centuriō erat versipellis.'

fābula	*story*
mīrābilis	*extraordinary, strange*
5 mīsit	*sent*
discessit	*departed, left*
pōculum hausit	*drained his wine-cup*
ex urbe	*from the city*
10 nox erat	*it was night*
lūna plēna	*full moon*
lūcēbat	*was shining*
silva	*wood*
centuriōnem	*centurion*
15 cōnspexit	*caught sight of*
dīxit	*said*
tunicam	*tunic*
dēposuit	*took off*
ēvānuit	*vanished*
lupus	*wolf*
appāruit	*appeared*
ululāvit	*howled*
cautē	*cautiously*
īnspexit	*looked at, examined*
lapidea	*made of stone*
rem intellēxit	*understood the truth*
versipellis	*werewolf*

About the language 1

1 Study the following example:

> mercātor Caecilium vīsitābat. mercātor vīllam intrāvit.
> *A merchant was visiting Caecilius. The merchant entered the house.*

2 In Stage 7, you have met a shorter way of saying this:

> mercātor Caecilium vīsitābat. vīllam intrāvit.
> *A merchant was visiting Caecilius.* **He** *entered the house.*

The following sentences behave in the same way:

> amīcī cum Caeciliō cēnābant. coquum laudāvērunt.
> *Friends were dining with Caecilius.* **They** *praised the cook.*

> ancilla in ātriō stābat. dominum salūtāvit.
> *The slave-girl was standing in the atrium.* **She** *greeted the master.*

3 Notice that Latin does not have to include a separate word for 'he', 'she' or 'they'. **intrāvit** can mean 'he entered' or 'she entered', depending on the context.

4 Further examples:

a Grumiō in culīnā labōrābat. cēnam parābat.
b āctōrēs in theātrō clāmābant. fābulam agēbant.
c Metella nōn erat in vīllā. in hortō ambulābat.
d lībertī in tabernā bibēbant. Grumiōnem salūtāvērunt.
e iuvenis pōculum hausit. vīnum laudāvit.

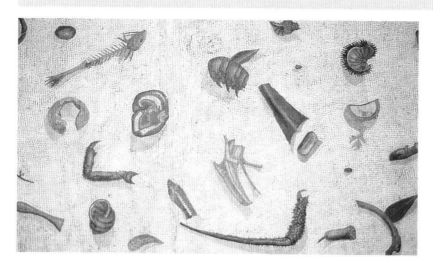

Part of a mosaic floor, showing the scraps left behind by the diners after a cena.

Decēns

postquam Fēlīx fābulam nārrāvit, Caecilius et hospitēs plausērunt. tum omnēs tacēbant et aliam fābulam exspectābant. subitō clāmōrem audīvērunt. omnēs ad ātrium festīnāvērunt, ubi Clēmēns stābat.

Caecilius:	hercle! quid est? cūr tū clāmōrem facis?
Clēmēns:	Decēns, Decēns…
Caecilius:	quid est?
Clēmēns:	Decēns est mortuus.
omnēs:	quid? mortuus? ēheu!
	(duo servī intrant.)
Caecilius:	quid dīcis?
servus prīmus:	dominus meus ad vīllam tuam veniēbat; dominus gladiātōrem prope amphitheātrum cōnspexit.
servus secundus:	gladiātor dominum terruit, quod gladium ingentem vibrābat. tum gladiātor clāmāvit,'tū mē nōn terrēs, leō, tū mē nōn terrēs! leōnēs amīcum meum in arēnā necāvērunt, sed tū mē nōn terrēs!'
servus prīmus:	Decēns valdē timēbat. 'tū es īnsānus', inquit dominus. 'ego nōn sum leō. sum homō.'
servus secundus:	gladiātor tamen dominum ferōciter petīvit et eum ad amphitheātrum trāxit. dominus perterritus clāmāvit. Clēmēns clāmōrem audīvit. Clēmēns, quod fortis erat, amphitheātrum intrāvit. Decentem in arēnā cōnspexit. dominus meus erat mortuus.
Caecilius:	ego rem intellegō! gladiātor erat Pugnāx. Pugnāx erat gladiātor nōtissimus. Pugnāx ōlim in arēnā pugnābat, et leō Pugnācem necāvit. Pugnāx nōn vīvit; Pugnāx est umbra. umbra Decentem necāvit.

hospitēs *guests*
plausērunt *applauded*
tacēbant *were silent*
aliam *another*
hercle! *by Hercules! good heavens!*

mortuus *dead*

5

prīmus *first* — 10
gladiātōrem *gladiator*
prope amphitheātrum *near the amphitheatre*
secundus *second*
terruit *frightened* — 15
gladium *sword*
vibrābat *was brandishing, was waving*
in arēnā *in the arena*
īnsānus *mad, crazy* — 20
homō *human being, man*
eum *him*
trāxit *dragged*

25

nōtissimus *very well-known*

vīvit *is alive* — 30
umbra *ghost*

Decēns valdē timēbat.

post cēnam

postquam Caecilius rem explicāvit, omnēs amīcī tacēbant. mox 'valē' dīxērunt et ē vīllā discessērunt. per viam timidē prōcēdēbant. nūllae stēllae lūcēbant. nūlla lūna erat in caelō. amīcī nihil audīvērunt, quod viae dēsertae erant. amīcī per urbem tacitē prōcēdēbant, quod umbram timēbant.

5

explicāvit *explained*
valē *goodbye*
timidē *nervously*
prōcēdēbant *were proceeding,
were advancing*
nūllae stēllae *no stars*
in caelō *in the sky*
dēsertae *deserted*

subitō fēlēs ululāvit. amīcī valdē timēbant. omnēs per urbem perterritī ruērunt, quod dē vītā dēspērābant. clāmōrem mīrābilem fēcērunt. multī Pompēiānī erant sollicitī, quod clāmōrem audīvērunt. Caecilius tamen clāmōrem nōn audīvit, quod in cubiculō dormiēbat.

10

fēlēs *cat*
ruērunt *rushed*
dē vītā dēspērābant *were in
despair of their lives*
fēcērunt *made*
sollicitī *worried, anxious*

About the language 2

1   In Stage 6, you met examples of the perfect tense. They looked
    like this:

> senex ad tabernam **ambulāvit.**   amīcī in urbe **dormīvērunt.**
> *The old man walked to the inn.*   *The friends slept in the city.*

This is a very common way of forming the perfect tense in Latin.

2   In Stage 7, you have met other forms of the perfect tense. Look at the
    following examples:

PRESENT	PERFECT	
	singular	*plural*
apparet	appāruit *s/he appeared*	appāruērunt *they appeared*
dīcit	dīxit *s/he said*	dīxērunt *they said*
discēdit	discessit *s/he left*	discessērunt *they left*
facit	fēcit *s/he made*	fēcērunt *they made*

3   If you are not sure whether a particular verb is in the present tense
    or the perfect tense, you can check by looking it up in the 'Vocabulary'
    part of the Language information section.

Metella et Melissa

Metella Melissam in vīllā quaerēbat. Metella culīnam intrāvit,
ubi Grumiō labōrābat. Grumiō erat īrātus.

'cūr tū es īrātus, Grumiō? cūr ferōciter circumspectās?'
rogāvit Metella.

'heri Melissa cēnam optimam parāvit', respondit coquus.
'hodiē ego cēnam pessimam parō, quod nūllus cibus adest. heri
multus cibus erat in culīnā. ancilla omnem cibum coxit.'

Metella ē culīnā discessit et ad tablīnum festīnāvit, ubi
Clēmēns labōrābat. Clēmēns quoque erat īrātus.

'Melissa est pestis!' clāmāvit servus.

'quid fēcit Melissa?' rogāvit Metella.

'heri Melissa in tablīnō labōrābat', respondit Clēmēns. 'hodiē
ego in tablīnō labōrō. ecce! cērae et stilī absunt. nihil est in locō
propriō.'

Metella, postquam ē tablīnō discessit, hortum intrāvit.
Metella Melissam in hortō vīdit. ēheu! ancilla lacrimābat.

'Melissa, cūr lacrimās?' rogāvit Metella.

'lacrimō quod Grumiō et Clēmēns mē vituperant', respondit
ancilla.

'ego tamen tē nōn vituperō', inquit Metella. 'ego tē laudō.
ecce! tū crīnēs meōs optimē compōnis. stolam meam optimē
compōnis. fortasse Grumiō et Clēmēns tē nōn laudant; sed ego
tē laudō, quod mē dīligenter cūrās.'

5 **heri** *yesterday*
pessimam *very bad*
coxit *cooked*

10

fēcit *has done*

stilī *pens (used for writing*
                           on wax tablets)
15 **in locō propriō** *in the right*
                           place
vīdit *saw*

20

crīnēs *hair*
optimē *very well*
compōnis *arrange*
stolam *dress*
fortasse *perhaps*
dīligenter *carefully*
cūrās *look after*

Practising the language

1 Complete each sentence with the right phrase. Then translate the sentence.

> For example: amīcī . . . . (vīllam intrāvit, cēnam laudāvērunt)
> **amīcī cēnam laudāvērunt.**
> *The friends praised the dinner.*

a mercātor . . . . (ē vīllā discessit, clāmōrem audīvērunt)
b ancillae . . . . (ad vīllam ambulāvit, in vīllā dormīvērunt)
c leōnēs . . . . (gladiātōrem terruit, gladiātōrem cōnspexērunt)
d lībertī . . . . (lūnam spectāvit, ad portum festīnāvērunt)
e centuriō . . . . (fābulam audīvit, servum laudāvērunt)
f fūr . . . . (per urbem ruit, centuriōnem terruērunt)
g Caecilius et amīcus . . . . (leōnem cōnspexit, portum petīvērunt)
h amīcī . . . . (pōculum īnspexit, rem intellēxērunt)

2 Complete each sentence with the right form of the noun. Then translate the sentence.

> For example: coquus . . . . . . parāvit. (cēna, cēnam)
> coquus **cēnam** parāvit.
> *The cook prepared the dinner.*
>
> . . . . . . ad silvam ambulāvērunt. (servus, servī)
> **servī** ad silvam ambulāvērunt.
> *The slaves walked to the wood.*

a Clēmēns . . . . . . excitāvit. (dominus, dominum)
b . . . . . . fābulam nārrāvit. (lībertus, lībertum)
c . . . . . gladiātōrem cōnspexērunt. (amīcus, amīcī)
d . . . . . . ad forum festīnāvērunt. (agricola, agricolae)
e ancilla . . . . . . aperuit. (iānua, iānuam)
f . . . . . . clāmōrem fēcit. (puella, puellae)
g fūrēs . . . . . . necāvērunt. (centuriō, centuriōnem)
h . . . . . . cēnam laudāvit. (gladiātor, gladiātōrem)
i . . . . . . cibum ad theātrum portāvērunt. (spectātor, spectātōrēs)
j . . . . . . ē vīllā discessit. (senex, senēs)

Tombs outside the Herculaneum Gate.

Roman beliefs about life after death

The Romans usually placed the tombs of the dead by the side of roads just outside towns. The tombs at Pompeii can still be seen along the roads that go north from the Herculaneum Gate and south from the Nuceria Gate.

Some tombs were grand and impressive and looked like small houses; others were plain and simple. Inside a tomb there was a chest or vase containing the ashes of the dead person; sometimes there were recesses in the walls of a tomb to hold the remains of several members of a family. The ashes of poor people, who could not afford the expense of a tomb, were buried more simply. At this time cremation was the normal way of disposing of the dead.

In building their cemeteries along busy roads, and not in peaceful and secluded places, the Romans were not showing any lack of respect. On the contrary, they believed that unless the dead were properly treated, their ghosts would haunt the living and possibly do them harm. It was most important to provide the dead with a tomb or grave, where their ghosts could have a home. But it was also thought that they would want to be close to the life of the living. One tomb has this inscription: 'I see and gaze upon all who come to and from the city' and another, 'Lollius has been placed by the side of the road in order that everyone who passes may say to him "Hello, Lollius"'.

Inside a Pompeian tomb, with recesses for the ashes.

It was believed that the dead in some way continued the activities of life, and therefore had to be supplied with the things they would need. A craftsman would want his tools, a woman her jewellery, children their toys. When the bodies of the dead were cremated, their possessions were burnt or buried with them.

A Greek writer called Lucian tells the story of a husband who had burnt all his dead wife's jewellery and clothes on the funeral pyre, so that she might have them in the next world. A week later he was trying to comfort himself by reading a book about life after death, when the ghost of his wife appeared. She began to reproach him because he had not burnt one of her gilt sandals, which, she said, was lying under a chest. The family dog then barked and the ghost disappeared. The husband looked under the chest, found the sandal and burnt it. The ghost was now content and did not appear again.

The ghosts of the dead were also thought to be hungry and thirsty, and therefore had to be given food and drink. Offerings of eggs, beans, lentils, flour and wine were placed regularly at the tomb. Sometimes holes were made in the tomb so that food and wine could be poured inside. Wine was a convenient substitute for blood, the favourite drink of the dead. At the funeral and on special occasions animals were sacrificed, and their blood was offered.

Section through a Roman burial in Caerleon, Wales. A pipe ran down into the container for the ashes, so that gifts of food and drink could be poured in.

Cremation urns

Ashes were buried in containers of many materials, including stone, metal and glass. One wealthy Pompeian had his ashes buried in this fabulously expensive, hand-carved blue and white glass vase, which was found in one of the tombs outside the Herculaneum Gate. Poor people might put the ashes of the dead in second-hand storage jars which were then buried in the earth.

It was thought, however, that in spite of these attempts to look after them, the dead did not lead a very happy existence. In order to help them forget their unhappiness, their tombs were often decorated with flowers and surrounded by little gardens, a custom which has lasted to this day, although its original meaning has changed. With the same purpose in mind, the family and friends of a dead person held a banquet after the funeral and on the anniversary of the death. Sometimes these banquets took place in a dining-room attached to the tomb itself, sometimes in the family home. The ghosts of the dead were thought to attend and enjoy these cheerful occasions.

In addition to these ceremonies two festivals for the dead were held every year. At one of these, families remembered

Left: *An open-air dining-room attached to a tomb outside the Herculaneum Gate, where the relatives could feast with the dead.*

parents and relations who had died; at the other, they performed rites to exorcise any ghosts in their houses who might be lonely or hungry and therefore dangerous.

Some people also believed in the Greek myths about the underworld where the wicked were punished for their crimes and where the good lived happily for ever.

There were a few people who did not believe in any form of life after death. These were the followers of a Greek philosopher called Epicurus, who taught that when a man died the breath that gave him life dissolved in the air and was lost for ever.

Most Romans, however, felt no need to question their traditional beliefs and customs, which kept the dead alive in their memories and ensured that their spirits were happy and at peace.

A bronze head of Epicurus, from a villa at Herculaneum.

Vocabulary checklist 7

cēnat	dines
cōnspicit	catches sight of
cum	with
facit	makes, does
heri	yesterday
ingēns	huge
intellegit	understands
lacrimat	weeps, cries
mortuus	dead
nārrat	tells, relates
necat	kills
nihil	nothing
omnis	all
parat	prepares
prope	near
rogat	asks
tacitē	quietly
tamen	however
terret	frightens
valdē	very much

Dead sinners being punished in the underworld: Sisyphus had to roll a stone for ever, Ixion was tied to a revolving wheel, and Tantalus was never able to quench his raging thirst.

GLADIATORES

STAGE 8

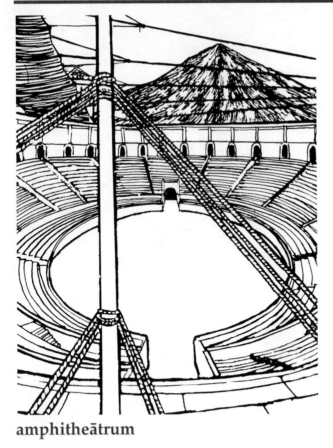

amphitheātrum

1 nūntiī spectāculum nūntiābant.
Pompēiānī nūntiōs audiēbant.

2 gladiātōrēs per viam prōcēdēbant.
Pompēiānī gladiātōrēs laudābant.

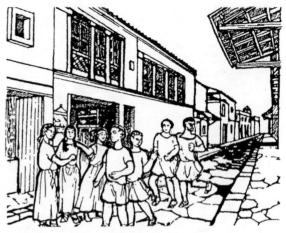

3 puellae iuvenēs salūtāvērunt. iuvenēs
quoque ad amphitheātrum contendēbant.

4 servī fēminās spectābant, quod fēminae
  ad spectāculum contendēbant.

5 puerī per viam festīnābant. puellae puerōs
  salūtāvērunt.

6 Pompēiānī tabernās nōn intrāvērunt,
  quod tabernae erant clausae.

7 postquam gladiātōrēs Pompēiānōs
  salūtāvērunt, Pompēiānī plausērunt.

8 Pompēiānī gladiātōrēs intentē spectābant,
  quod gladiātōrēs in arēnā pugnābant.

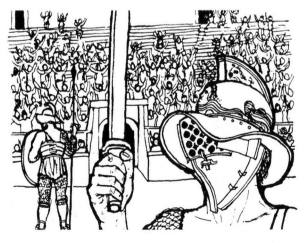

9 spectātōrēs murmillōnēs incitābant, quod
  murmillōnēs saepe victōrēs erant.

gladiātōrēs

Rēgulus erat senātor Rōmānus. in vīllā magnificā habitābat. vīlla erat prope Nūceriam. Nūcerīnī et Pompēiānī erant inimīcī. Nūcerīnī, quod amphitheātrum nōn habēbant, saepe ad amphitheātrum Pompēiānum veniēbant; saepe erant turbulentī.

Rēgulus ōlim spectāculum splendidum in amphitheātrō ēdidit, quod diem nātālem celebrābat. multī Nūcerīnī igitur ad urbem vēnērunt. cīvēs Pompēiānī erant īrātī, quod Nūcerīnī viās complēbant. omnēs tamen ad forum contendērunt, ubi nūntiī stābant. nūntiī spectāculum optimum nūntiābant:

'gladiātōrēs adsunt! vīgintī gladiātōrēs hodiē pugnant! rētiāriī adsunt! murmillōnēs adsunt! bēstiāriī bēstiās ferōcēs agitant!'

Pompēiānī, postquam nūntiōs audīvērunt, ad amphitheātrum quam celerrimē contendērunt. Nūcerīnī quoque ad amphitheātrum festīnāvērunt. omnēs vehementer clāmābant. Pompēiānī et Nūcerīnī, postquam amphitheātrum intrāvērunt, tacuērunt. prīmam pugnam exspectābant.

senātor Rōmānus	*a Roman senator*
magnificā	*magnificent*
Nūcerīnī	*the people of Nuceria*
inimīcī	*enemies*
saepe	*often*
turbulentī	*rowdy, disorderly*
spectāculum	*show, spectacle*
splendidum	*splendid*
ēdidit	*presented*
diem nātālem	*birthday*
celebrābat	*was celebrating*
vēnērunt	*came*
cīvēs	*citizens*
complēbant	*were filling*
nūntiābant	*were announcing*
vīgintī	*twenty*
rētiāriī	*net-fighters*
murmillōnēs	*heavily armed gladiators*
bēstiāriī	*beast-fighters*
bēstiās	*beasts*
ferōcēs	*fierce, ferocious*
quam celerrimē	*as quickly as possible*
vehementer	*loudly, violently*
tacuērunt	*fell silent*

The amphitheatre at Pompeii. Notice one of the staircases that led up to the top seats. The public sports ground is behind the trees on the right. On performance days, the open space would have been full of stalls selling refreshments and souvenirs.

A retiarius with his trident, net and protection for his right arm and neck.

in arēnā

duo rētiāriī et duo murmillōnēs arēnam intrāvērunt. postquam
gladiātōrēs spectātōrēs salūtāvērunt, tuba sonuit. tum
gladiātōrēs pugnam commīsērunt. murmillōnēs Pompēiānōs
valdē dēlectābant, quod saepe victōrēs erant. Pompēiānī igitur
murmillōnēs incitābant. sed rētiāriī, quod erant expedītī,   5
murmillōnēs facile ēvītāvērunt.

    'rētiāriī nōn pugnant! rētiāriī sunt ignāvī!' clāmāvērunt
Pompēiānī. Nūcerīnī tamen respondērunt, 'rētiāriī sunt callidī!
rētiāriī murmillōnēs dēcipiunt!'

    murmillōnēs rētiāriōs frūstrā ad pugnam prōvocāvērunt. tum   10
murmillō clāmāvit, 'ūnus murmillō facile duōs rētiāriōs superat.'

    Pompēiānī plausērunt. tum murmillō rētiāriōs statim petīvit.
murmillō et rētiāriī ferōciter pugnāvērunt. rētiāriī tandem
murmillōnem graviter vulnerāvērunt. tum rētiāriī alterum
murmillōnem petīvērunt. hic murmillō fortiter pugnāvit, sed   15
rētiāriī eum quoque superāvērunt.

    Pompēiānī, quod īrātī erant, murmillōnēs vituperābant;
missiōnem tamen postulābant, quod murmillōnēs fortēs erant.
Nūcerīnī mortem postulābant. omnēs spectātōrēs tacēbant, et
Rēgulum intentē spectābant. Rēgulus, quod Nūcerīnī mortem   20
postulābant, pollicem vertit. Pompēiānī erant īrātī, et
vehementer clāmābant. rētiāriī tamen, postquam Rēgulus
signum dedit, murmillōnēs interfēcērunt.

tuba *trumpet*
sonuit *sounded*
pugnam commīsērunt *began the fight*
victōrēs *victors, winners*
expedītī *lightly armed*
ēvītāvērunt *avoided*
ignāvī *cowardly*
callidī *clever, cunning*
dēcipiunt *are deceiving, are fooling*
frūstrā *in vain*
prōvocāvērunt *challenged*
ūnus *one*
graviter *seriously*
vulnerāvērunt *wounded*
alterum *the second, the other*
hic *this*
fortiter *bravely*
missiōnem *release*
mortem *death*
pollicem vertit *turned his thumb up*
dedit *gave*
interfēcērunt *killed*

About the language 1

1   From Stage 2 onwards, you have met sentences like these:

> amīcus **puellam** salūtat.   *The friend greets the girl.*
> dominus **servum** vituperābat.   *The master was cursing the slave.*
> nautae **mercātōrem** laudāvērunt.   *The sailors praised the merchant.*

In each of these examples, the person who has something done to him or her is indicated in Latin by the **accusative singular.**

2   In Stage 8, you have met sentences like these:

> amīcus **puellās** salūtat.   *The friend greets the girls.*
> dominus **servōs** vituperābat.   *The master was cursing the slaves.*
> nautae **mercātōrēs** laudāvērunt.   *The sailors praised the merchants.*

In these examples, the persons who have something done to them are indicated in Latin by the **accusative plural.**

3   You have now met the following cases:

SINGULAR			
nominative	puella	servus	mercātor
accusative	puellam	servum	mercātōrem

PLURAL			
nominative	puellae	servī	mercātōrēs
accusative	puellās	servōs	mercātōrēs

4   Further examples:

a   agricola gladiātōrem laudāvit. agricola gladiātōrēs laudāvit.
b   servus agricolam interfēcit. servus agricolās interfēcit.
c   centuriō servōs laudāvit.
d   puer āctōrēs ad theātrum dūxit.
e   senex āctōrem ad forum dūxit.
f   amīcus fābulās nārrāvit.
g   amīcī ancillam salūtāvērunt.
h   agricolae nūntiōs audīvērunt.

vēnātiō

vēnātiō   *hunt*

When you have read this story, answer the questions at the end.

postquam rētiāriī ex arēnā discessērunt, tuba iterum sonuit.
subitō multī cervī arēnam intrāvērunt. cervī per tōtam arēnam
currēbant, quod perterritī erant. tum canēs ferōcēs per portam
intrāvērunt. canēs statim cervōs perterritōs agitāvērunt et
interfēcērunt. postquam canēs cervōs superāvērunt, lupī arēnam   5
intrāvērunt. lupī, quod valdē ēsuriēbant, canēs ferōciter
petīvērunt. canēs erant fortissimī, sed lupī facile canēs
superāvērunt.

    Nūcerīnī erant laetissimī et Rēgulum laudābant. Pompēiānī
tamen nōn erant contentī, sed clāmābant, 'ubi sunt leōnēs? cūr   10
Rēgulus leōnēs retinet?'

    Rēgulus, postquam hunc clāmōrem audīvit, signum dedit.
statim trēs leōnēs per portam ruērunt. tuba iterum sonuit. bēstiāriī
arēnam audācissimē intrāvērunt. leōnēs tamen bēstiāriōs nōn
petīvērunt. leōnēs in arēnā recubuērunt. leōnēs obdormīvērunt!   15

    tum Pompēiānī erant īrātissimī, quod Rēgulus spectāculum
rīdiculum ēdēbat. Pompēiānī Rēgulum et Nūcerīnōs ex
amphitheātrō agitāvērunt. Nūcerīnī per viās fugiēbant, quod
valdē timēbant. Pompēiānī tamen gladiōs suōs dēstrīnxērunt et
multōs Nūcerīnōs interfēcērunt. ecce! sanguis nōn in arēnā sed   20
per viās fluēbat.

Glossary (margin):

iterum *again*
cervī *deer*

ēsuriēbant *were hungry*
fortissimī *very brave*

retinet *is holding back*
hunc *this*
trēs *three*
audācissimē *very boldly*
recubuērunt *lay down*
obdormīvērunt *went to sleep*
īrātissimī *very angry*
rīdiculum *ridiculous, silly*
ēdēbat *was presenting*
fugiēbant *began to run away, began to flee*

suōs *their*
dēstrīnxērunt *drew*

Questions

		Marks
1	**postquam … intrāvērunt** (lines 1–2). What happened after the retiarii left the arena?	2
2	In lines 4–5, how did the deer feel and what happened to them?	1 + 2
3	In lines 6–8, why did the wolves chase the dogs? How did the chase end?	2
4	In lines 9–10, what were the different feelings of the Nucerians and Pompeians?	2
5	Why were the Pompeians feeling like this?	1
6	**Rēgulus … signum dedit** (line 12). What happened next?	2
7	When the beast-fighters entered the arena in lines 13–14, what would you have expected to happen? What went wrong?	2 + 1
8	Why were the Pompeians angry and what did they do?	2
9	**Pompēiānī … interfēcērunt** (lines 19–20). What made the riot so serious?	1
10	Read the last sentence. Why do you think **ecce!** is put in front of it?	2

TOTAL   **20**

pāstor et leō

ōlim pāstor in silvā ambulābat. subitō pāstor leōnem cōnspexit.
leō tamen pāstōrem nōn agitāvit. leō lacrimābat! pāstor,
postquam leōnem cōnspexit, erat attonitus et rogāvit,

    'cūr lacrimās, leō? cūr mē nōn agitās? cūr mē nōn cōnsūmis?'

    leō trīstis pedem ostendit. pāstor spīnam in pede cōnspexit,
tum clāmāvit,

    'ego spīnam videō! spīnam ingentem videō! nunc intellegō!
tū lacrimās, quod pēs dolet.'

    pāstor, quod benignus et fortis erat, ad leōnem cautē vēnit et
spīnam īnspexit. leō fremuit, quod ignāvus erat.

    'leō!' exclāmāvit pāstor, 'ego perterritus sum, quod tū fremis.
sed tē adiuvō. ecce! spīna!'

    postquam hoc dīxit, pāstor spīnam quam celerrimē extrāxit.
leō ignāvus iterum fremuit et ē silvā festīnāvit.

    posteā, Rōmānī hunc pāstōrem comprehendērunt, quod
Chrīstiānus erat, et eum ad arēnam dūxērunt. postquam arēnam
intrāvit, pāstor spectātōrēs vīdit et valdē timēbat. tum pāstor
bēstiās vīdit et clāmāvit, 'nunc mortuus sum! videō leōnēs et
lupōs. ēheu!'

    tum ingēns leō ad eum ruit. leō, postquam pāstōrem olfēcit,
nōn eum cōnsūmpsit sed lambēbat! pāstor attonitus leōnem
agnōvit et dīxit,

    'tē agnōscō! tū es leō trīstis! spīna erat in pede tuō.'

    leō iterum fremuit, et pāstōrem ex arēnā ad salūtem dūxit.

	attonitus *astonished*
5	**trīstis** *sad*
	pedem *foot, paw*
	ostendit *showed*
	spīnam *thorn*
	dolet *hurts*
10	**benignus** *kind*
	fremuit *roared*
	exclāmāvit *shouted*
	adiuvō *help*
	hoc *this*
15	**extrāxit** *pulled out*
	posteā *afterwards*
	comprehendērunt *arrested*
	Chrīstiānus *Christian*
20	**olfēcit** *smelled, sniffed*
	lambēbat *began to lick*
	agnōvit *recognised*
	ad salūtem *to safety*

About the language 2

1   Study the following pairs of sentences:

Pompēiānī erant īrātī.
The Pompeians were angry.

Pompēiānī erant **īrātissimī.**
The Pompeians were very angry.

gladiātor est nōtus.
The gladiator is famous.

gladiātor est **nōtissimus.**
The gladiator is very famous.

māter erat laeta.
The mother was happy.

māter erat **laetissima.**
The mother was very happy.

The words in **bold type** are known as **superlatives.** Notice how they are translated in the examples above.

2   Further examples:

a   mercātor est trīstis. senex est trīstissimus.
b   canis erat ferōx. leō erat ferōcissimus.
c   amīcus fābulam longissimam nārrāvit.
d   murmillōnēs erant fortēs, sed rētiāriī erant fortissimī.

A duel reaches its climax in this painting from a tomb at Pompeii.

Practising the language

1   Complete each sentence with the right word from the box.
    Then translate the sentence.

    a   . . . . . . multās vīllās habeō.
    b   ego servōs . . . .
    c   tū gladiātōrēs . . . .
    d   ego . . . . . . salūtō.
    e   . . . . . . ancillās laudās.
    f   tū . . . . . . agitās.

ego	leōnēs
tū	vēndō
amīcōs	spectās

2   Complete each sentence with the right form of the verb from the brackets.
    Then translate the sentence.

    a   tū es vēnālīcius; tū servōs in forō . . . . (vēndō, vēndis, vēndit)
    b   ego sum gladiātor; ego in arēnā . . . . (pugnō, pugnās, pugnat)
    c   Fēlīx est lībertus; Fēlīx cum Caeciliō . . . . (cēnō, cēnās, cēnat)
    d   ego multōs spectātōrēs in amphitheātrō . . . . (videō, vidēs, videt)
    e   tū in vīllā magnificā . . . . (habitō, habitās, habitat)
    f   Rēgulus hodiē diem nātālem . . . . (celebrō, celebrās, celebrat)
    g   tū saepe ad amphitheātrum . . . . (veniō, venīs, venit)
    h   ego rem . . . . (intellegō, intellegis, intellegit)

*Gladiator fights were show
business, and were performed to
the sound of trumpet and organ.*

Gladiatorial shows

The inside of the Pompeii amphitheatre as it is today, looking north-west towards Vesuvius. Compare the drawing on page 111. The building held about 20,000 people and the number of seats was being increased when the city was destroyed.

Among the most popular entertainments in all parts of the Roman world were shows in which gladiators fought each other. These contests were usually held in an amphitheatre. This was a large oval building, without a roof, in which rising tiers of seats surrounded an arena. Canvas awnings, supported by ropes and pulleys, were spread over part of the seating area to give shelter from the sun. The amphitheatre at Pompeii was large enough to contain the whole population as well as many visitors from nearby towns. Spectators paid no admission fee, as the shows were given by wealthy individuals at their own expense.

Among the many advertisements for gladiatorial shows that are to be seen painted on the walls of buildings is this one:

> Twenty pairs of gladiators, given by Lucretius Satrius Valens, priest of Nero, and ten pairs of gladiators provided by his son will fight at Pompeii from 8 to 12 April. There will also be an animal hunt. Awnings will be provided.

Soon after dawn on the day of a show, the spectators would begin to take their places. A trumpet blared and priests came out to perform the religious ceremony with which the games began. Then the gladiators entered in procession, paraded round the arena and saluted the sponsor of the show. The gladiators were then paired off to fight each other and the contests began.

Bird's-eye view of the amphitheatre showing the awning.

The gladiators were slaves, condemned criminals, prisoners of war or free volunteers; they lived and trained in a 'school' or barracks under the supervision of a professional trainer.

Part of the programme of one particular show, together with details of the results, reads as follows:

> A Thracian versus a Murmillo
> Won: Pugnax from Nero's school: 3 times a winner
> Died: Murranus from Nero's school: 3 times a winner
>
> A Heavily-armed Gladiator versus a Thracian
> Won: Cycnus from the school of Julius: 8 times a winner
> Allowed to live: Atticus from the school of Julius:
> 14 times a winner
>
> Chariot Fighters
> Won: Scylax from the school of Julius: 26 times a winner
> Allowed to live: Publius Ostorius: 51 times a winner

The fight ended with the death or surrender of one of the gladiators. The illustrations below, based on a relief from the tomb of a wealthy Pompeian, show the defeated gladiator appealing to the spectators; the victor stands by ready to kill him if they decide that he deserves to die. Notice the arm raised in appeal. The spectators indicated their wishes by turning their thumbs up or down: probably turning the thumb up towards the chest meant 'kill him', while turning it down meant 'let him live'. The final decision for death or mercy was made by the sponsor of the show. It was not unusual for the life of the loser to be spared, especially if he were a well-known gladiator with a good number of victories to his credit. The most successful gladiators were great favourites with the crowd and received gifts of money from their admirers. One popular Pompeian

Gladiators' armour

Gladiators were not all armed in the same way. Some, who were known as Samnites, carried an oblong shield and a short sword; others, known as Thracians, had a round shield and a curved sword or dagger. Another type of gladiator armed with sword and shield wore a helmet with a crest shaped like a fish; the Greek name for the fish was 'mormillos' and the gladiator was known as a murmillō. *The murmillones were often matched against the* rētiāriī *who were armed with* rētia *(nets) and three-pronged tridents.*

Other types of gladiator fought with spears, on horseback, or from chariots. Occasionally women gladiators were used, bringing additional variety to the show.

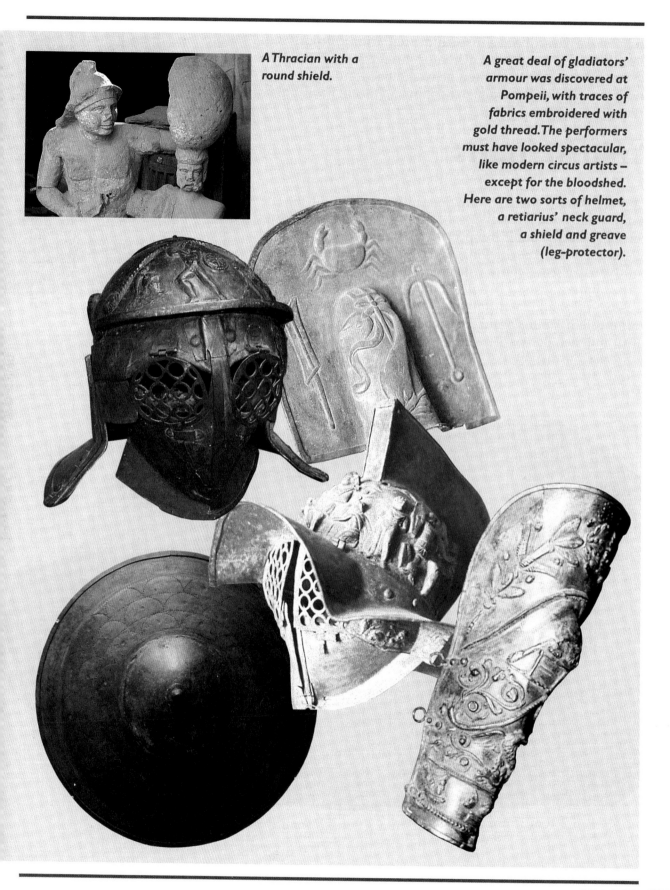

A Thracian with a round shield.

A great deal of gladiators' armour was discovered at Pompeii, with traces of fabrics embroidered with gold thread. The performers must have looked spectacular, like modern circus artists – except for the bloodshed. Here are two sorts of helmet, a retiarius' neck guard, a shield and greave (leg-protector).

gladiator was described as **suspīrium puellārum**: 'the girls' heart-throb'. Eventually, if a gladiator survived long enough or showed great skill and courage, he would be awarded the wooden sword. This was a high honour and meant he would not have to fight again.

Animal hunts

Many shows also offered a **vēnātiō**, a hunt of wild animals. The **bēstiae** (wild beasts) were released from cages into the arena, where they were hunted by specially trained beast-fighters called **bēstiāriī.** In the drawing on the right, taken from the same tomb, you can see a wolf, a wild boar, a bull, hares and a lion.

The hunters, who wore light clothing, relied only upon a thrusting spear and their agility to avoid injury. By the end of the hunt all the animals and occasionally a few hunters had been killed, and their bodies were dragged out from the sandy floor of the arena to be disposed of.

The riot at Pompeii

The story told in this Stage is based on an actual event which occurred in AD 59. In addition to the evidence given in the wall-painting above, the event is also described by the Roman historian Tacitus in these words:

> About this time, a slight incident led to a serious outburst of rioting between the people of Pompeii and Nuceria. It occurred at a show of gladiators, sponsored by Livineius Regulus. While hurling insults at each other, in the usual manner of country people, they suddenly began to throw stones as well. Finally, they drew swords and attacked each other. The men of Pompeii won the fight. As a result, most of the families of Nuceria lost a father or a son. Many of the wounded were taken to Rome, where the Emperor Nero requested the Senate to hold an inquiry. After the inquiry, the Senate forbade the Pompeians to hold such shows for ten years. Livineius and others who had encouraged the riot were sent into exile.

This drawing of a gladiator with the palm of victory was scratched on a wall, with a message that may refer to the riot and its aftermath: 'Campanians, in your moment of victory you perished along with the Nucerians'.

Vocabulary checklist 8

agitat	chases, hunts
cōnsūmit	eats
dūcit	leads, takes
eum	him
facile	easily
ferōx	fierce
gladius	sword
hic	this
ignāvus	cowardly
nūntius	messenger
pēs	foot
porta	gate
postulat	demands
puer	boy
pugnat	fights
saepe	often
sanguis	blood
silva	wood
spectāculum	show, spectacle
statim	at once
tōtus	whole

A retiarius who lost his fight. The symbol beside his trident is θ (theta), the first letter of the Greek word for death (thanatos).

THERMAE

STAGE 9

1 Quīntus ad thermās vēnit.

2 Quīntus servō pecūniam dedit.

3 amīcī Quīntum laetē salūtāvērunt, quod
diem nātālem celebrābat.

4 Quīntus discum novum ferēbat. Quīntus
amīcīs discum ostendit.

5 postquam Quīntus discum ēmīsit, discus
statuam percussit.

6 ēheu! statua nāsum frāctum habēbat.

7 Metella et Melissa in forō ambulābant.
Metella fīliō dōnum quaerēbat.

8 fēminae mercātōrem cōnspexērunt.
mercātor fēminīs togās ostendit.

9 Metella Quīntō togam ēlēgit. Melissa
mercātōrī pecūniam dedit.

10 Grumiō cēnam optimam in culīnā
parābat. coquus Quīntō cēnam parābat,
quod diem nātālem celebrābat.

11 multī hospitēs cum Quīntō cēnābant.
Clēmēns hospitibus vīnum offerēbat.

12 ancilla triclīnium intrāvit. Quīntus ancillae
signum dedit. ancilla suāviter cantāvit.

in palaestrā

When you have read this story, answer the questions opposite.

Caecilius Quīntō discum dedit, quod diem nātālem celebrābat.
tum Caecilius fīlium ad thermās dūxit, ubi palaestra erat. servus
Quīntō discum ferēbat.

Caecilius et fīlius, postquam thermās intrāvērunt, ad
palaestram contendērunt. turba ingēns in palaestrā erat. Quīntus   5
multōs iuvenēs et āthlētās cōnspexit. Quīntus multās statuās in
palaestrā vīdit.

'Pompēiānī āthlētīs nōtissimīs statuās posuērunt', inquit
Caecilius.

in palaestrā erat porticus ingēns. spectātōrēs in porticū   10
stābant. servī spectātōribus vīnum offerēbant.

Quīntus turbam prope porticum vīdit. āthlēta ingēns in
mediā turbā stābat.

'quis est āthlēta ille?' rogāvit Quīntus.

'ille est Milō, āthlēta nōtissimus', respondit Caecilius.   15

Caecilius et Quīntus ad Milōnem contendērunt.

Quīntus āthlētae discum novum ostendit. Milō, postquam
discum īnspexit, ad mediam palaestram prōcessit. āthlēta
palaestram circumspectāvit et discum ēmīsit. discus longē per
aurās ēvolāvit. spectātōrēs āthlētam laudāvērunt. servus Milōnī   20
discum quaesīvit. servus, postquam discum invēnit, ad
Milōnem rediit. servus āthlētae discum offerēbat. āthlēta tamen
discum nōn accēpit.

'discus nōn est meus', inquit Milō.

servus Quīntō discum trādidit. tum iuvenis quoque discum   25
ēmīsit. discus iterum per aurās ēvolāvit. discus tamen statuam
percussit.

'ēheu!' clāmāvit Caecilius. 'statua nāsum frāctum habet.'

Quīntus rīdēbat. Pompēiānī rīdēbant. Milō tamen nōn
rīdēbat.   30

'cūr tū nōn rīdēs?' rogāvit iuvenis.

Milō erat īrātissimus.

'pestis!' respondit āthlēta. 'mea est statua!'

---

in palaestrā *in the palaestra, in the exercise area*

discum *discus*
thermās *baths*
ferēbat *was carrying*

āthlētās *athletes*
statuās *statues*
posuērunt *have placed, have put up*

porticus *colonnade*
offerēbant *were offering*
in mediā turbā *in the middle of the crowd*
āthlēta ille *that athlete*

novum *new*
prōcessit *proceeded, advanced*
ēmīsit *threw*
longē *a long way, far*
per aurās ēvolāvit *flew through the air*
invēnit *found*
rediit *came back*
nōn accēpit *did not accept*
trādidit *handed over*
percussit *struck*
nāsum frāctum *a broken nose*

Questions

		Marks
1	Why did Caecilius give Quintus a discus?	1
2	Why do you think Caecilius took Quintus to the baths (lines 1–2)?	2
3	**turba ingēns in palaestrā erat** (line 5). Who were in the crowd?	1
4	Why were there statues in the palaestra?	2
5	Pick out two Latin words used in lines 12–15 to describe the athlete Milo. What do they tell us about him?	2
6	**āthlēta palaestram circumspectāvit** (lines 18–19). Why do you think Milo did this before throwing the discus?	2
7	How did the spectators react in line 20? Why did they react in this way?	2
8	**discus nōn est meus** (line 24). What had just happened to make Milo say this?	2
9	In lines 26–8, what happened when Quintus threw the discus?	2
10	How was Milo's reaction different from that of the Pompeians (lines 29–33)? Do you think he was right to behave as he did?	2 + 2
	TOTAL	20

The palaestra of the Stabian Baths at Pompeii.

About the language

1   Study the following examples:

Clēmēns **puellae** vīnum offerēbat.
*Clemens was offering wine **to the girl**.*

iuvenis **servō** pecūniam trādidit.
*The young man handed over money **to the slave**.*

dominus **mercātōrī** statuam ēmit.
*The master bought a statue **for the merchant**.*

Grumiō **ancillīs** cēnam parāvit.
*Grumio prepared a dinner **for the slave-girls**.*

Quīntus **amīcīs** discum ostendit.
*Quintus showed the discus **to his friends**.*

servī **leōnibus** cibum dedērunt.
*The slaves gave food **to the lions**.*

The words in **bold type** are nouns in the **dative case**.

2   You have now met three cases. Notice the different ways in which
they are used:

nominative   **servus** dormiēbat.
                  The slave was sleeping.

accusative   dominus **servum** excitāvit.
                  *The master woke **the slave**.*

dative   dominus **servō** signum dedit.
                  *The master gave a sign **to the slave**.*

3   Here is a full list of the noun endings that you have met.
The new dative cases are in **bold type**.

		first declension	second declension	third declension
SINGULAR	nominative	puella	servus	mercātor
	accusative	puellam	servum	mercātōrem
	dative	**puellae**	**servō**	**mercātōrī**
PLURAL	nominative	puellae	servī	mercātōrēs
	accusative	puellās	servōs	mercātōrēs
	dative	**puellīs**	**servīs**	**mercātōribus**

4   Further examples:

a   ancilla dominō cibum ostendit.
b   agricola uxōrī ānulum ēmit.
c   servus Metellae togam trādidit.
d   mercātor gladiātōribus pecūniam offerēbat.
e   fēmina ancillīs tunicās quaerēbat.

5   Notice the different cases of the words for 'I' and 'you':

nominative	ego	tū
accusative	mē	tē
dative	mihi	tibi

ego senem salūtō.   *I greet the old man.*
senex mē salūtat.   *The old man greets me.*
senex mihi statuam ostendit.   *The old man shows a statue to me.*

tū pictūram pingis.   *You are painting a picture.*
āthlēta tē laudat.   *The athlete praises you.*
āthlēta tibi pecūniam dat.   *The athlete gives money to you.*

in tabernā

Metella et Melissa ē vīllā māne discessērunt. Metella fīliō togam quaerēbat. Metella et ancilla, postquam forum intrāvērunt, tabernam cōnspexērunt, ubi togae optimae erant. multae fēminae erant in tabernā. servī fēminīs stolās ostendēbant. duo gladiātōrēs quoque in tabernā erant. servī gladiātōribus tunicās ostendēbant.

mercātor in mediā tabernā stābat. mercātor erat Marcellus. Marcellus, postquam Metellam vīdit, rogāvit,

'quid quaeris, domina?'

'togam quaerō', inquit Metella. 'ego fīliō dōnum quaerō, quod diem nātālem celebrat.'

'ego multās togās habeō', respondit mercātor.

mercātor servīs signum dedit. servī mercātōrī togās celeriter trādidērunt. Marcellus fēminīs togās ostendit. Metella et ancilla togās īnspexērunt.

'hercle!' clāmāvit Melissa. 'hae togae sunt sordidae.'

Marcellus servōs vituperāvit.

'sunt intus togae splendidae', inquit Marcellus.

Marcellus fēminās intus dūxit. mercātor fēminīs aliās togās ostendit. Metella Quīntō mox togam splendidam ēlēgit.

'haec toga, quantī est?' rogāvit Metella.

'quīnquāgintā dēnāriōs cupiō', respondit Marcellus.

'quīnquāgintā dēnāriōs cupis! furcifer!' clāmāvit Melissa. 'ego tibi decem dēnāriōs offerō.'

'quadrāgintā dēnāriōs cupiō', respondit mercātor.

'tibi quīndecim dēnāriōs offerō', inquit ancilla.

'quid? haec est toga pulcherrima! quadrāgintā dēnāriōs cupiō', respondit Marcellus.

'tū nimium postulās', inquit Metella. 'ego tibi trīgintā dēnāriōs dō.'

'cōnsentiō', respondit Marcellus.

Melissa Marcellō pecūniam dedit. Marcellus Metellae togam trādidit.

'ego tibi grātiās maximās agō, domina', inquit Marcellus.   35

---

māne *in the morning*
togam *toga*

domina *madam*
dōnum *present, gift*   10

hae togae *these togas*
sordidae *dirty*
intus *inside*   15
aliās *other*
ēlēgit *chose*
haec *this*
quantī est? *how much is it?*
quīnquāgintā dēnāriōs *fifty*   20
                                 denarii
cupiō *I want*
decem *ten*
quadrāgintā *forty*
quīndecim *fifteen*   25
pulcherrima *very beautiful*
nimium *too much*
trīgintā *thirty*
cōnsentiō *I agree*
ego tibi grātiās maximās agō   30
                         I thank you very much

A fabric shop.

Practising the language

1   Complete each sentence with the verb that makes good sense.
    Then translate the sentence, taking care with the different forms of the noun.

> For example: mercātōrēs fēminīs tunicās . . . . (audīvērunt, ostendērunt,
>   timuērunt)
>   mercātōrēs fēminīs tunicās **ostendērunt.**
>   *The merchants showed the tunics to the women.*

   a   ancilla dominō vīnum . . . . (timuit, dedit, salūtāvit)
   b   iuvenis puellae stolam . . . . . . (ēmit, vēnit, prōcessit)
   c   fēminae servīs tunicās . . . . . . (intrāvērunt, quaesīvērunt, contendērunt)
   d   cīvēs āctōrī pecūniam . . . . . . (laudāvērunt, vocāvērunt, trādidērunt)
   e   centuriō mercātōribus decem dēnāriōs . . . . . . (trādidit, ēmit, vīdit)

2   Complete each sentence with the right form of the verb. Then translate the sentence.

> For example: gladiātor amīcīs togam . . . . (ostendit, ostendērunt)
>   gladiātor amīcīs togam **ostendit.**
>   *The gladiator showed the toga to his friends.*

   a   puella gladiātōribus tunicās . . . . (dedit, dedērunt)
   b   cīvēs Milōnī statuam . . . . (posuit, posuērunt)
   c   mercātor amīcō vīnum . . . . (trādidit, trādidērunt)
   d   coquus ancillae ānulum . . . . . . (ēmit, ēmērunt)
   e   Clēmēns et Grumiō Metellae cēnam optimam . . . . . . (parāvit, parāvērunt)

3   This exercise is based on the story **in tabernā**, on page 120. Read the story again.
    Write out each sentence, completing it with the right noun or phrase. Then
    translate the sentence.

   a   Metella . . . . . . ad forum ambulāvit. (cum Quīntō, cum Grumiōne, cum Melissā)
   b   postquam forum intrāvērunt, ... cōnspexērunt. (portum, tabernam, vīllam)
   c   Metella gladiātōrēs et . . . . . . in tabernā vīdit. (āctōrēs, fēminās, centuriōnēs)
   d   servī fēminīs . . . . . . ostendēbant. (tunicās, stolās, togās)
   e   servī gladiātōribus . . . . . . ostendēbant. (togās, stolās, tunicās)
   f   mercātor servīs . . . . . . dedit. (signum, togam, gladium)
   g   servī mercātōrī . . . . . . trādidērunt. (togam, togās, stolās)
   h   mercātor . . . . . . vituperāvit, quod togae erant sordidae. (gladiātōrēs, fēminās, servōs)

in apodytēriō

duo servī in apodytēriō stant. servī sunt Sceledrus et Anthrāx.

Sceledrus:	cūr nōn labōrās, Anthrāx? num dormīs?
Anthrāx:	quid dīcis? dīligenter labōrō. ego cīvibus togās custōdiō.
Sceledrus:	togās custōdīs? mendāx es!
Anthrāx:	cūr mē vituperās? mendāx nōn sum. togās custōdiō.
Sceledrus:	tē vituperō, quod fūr est in apodytēriō, sed tū nihil facis.
Anthrāx:	ubi est fūr? fūrem nōn videō.
Sceledrus:	ecce! homō ille est fūr. fūrem facile agnōscō. *(Sceledrus Anthrācī fūrem ostendit. fūr togam suam dēpōnit et togam splendidam induit. servī ad fūrem statim currunt.)*
Anthrāx:	quid facis? furcifer! haec toga nōn est tua!
fūr:	mendāx es! mea est toga! abī!
Sceledrus:	tē agnōscō! pauper es, sed togam splendidam geris. *(mercātor intrat. togam frūstrā quaerit.)*
mercātor:	ēheu! ubi est toga mea? toga ēvānuit! *(mercātor circumspectat.)* ecce! hic fūr togam meam gerit!
fūr:	parce! parce! pauperrimus sum… uxor mea est aegra… decem līberōs habeō …

mercātor et servī fūrem nōn audiunt, sed eum ad iūdicem trahunt.

in apodytēriō *in the changing room*

5

num dormīs? *surely you are not asleep?*

10

suam *his*
induit *is putting on*

15

abī! *go away!*
pauper *poor*
geris *you are wearing*

20

parce! *spare me! have pity on me!*
pauperrimus *very poor*
aegra *sick, ill*
līberōs *children*
audiunt *listen to*

This mosaic of a squid is in an apodyterium in Herculaneum.

An apodyterium (changing-room) in the women's section of the Stabian Baths at Pompeii.

The caldarium (hot room) in the Forum Baths, Pompeii. At the nearer end note the large rectangular marble bath, which was filled with hot water. At the far end there is a stone basin for cold water. Rooms in baths often had grooved, curved ceilings to channel condensation down the walls.

The baths

About the middle of the afternoon, Caecilius would make his way, with a group of friends, to the public baths. The great majority of Pompeians did not have bathrooms in their houses, so they went regularly to the public baths to keep themselves clean. As in a leisure centre today, they could also take exercise, meet friends, and have a snack. Let us imagine that Caecilius decides to visit the baths situated just to the north of the forum, and let us follow him through the various rooms and activities.

At one of the entrances, he pays a small admission fee to the doorkeeper and then goes to the **palaestra** (exercise area). This is an open space surrounded by a colonnade, rather like a large peristylium. Here he spends a little time greeting other friends and taking part in some of the popular exercises, which included throwing a large ball from one to another, wrestling, and fencing with wooden swords. These games were not taken too seriously but were a pleasant preparation for the bath which followed.

From the palaestra, Caecilius and his friends walk along a passage into a large hall known as the **apodytērium** (changing-room). Here they undress and hand their clothes to one of the slave attendants who places them in recesses arranged in rows along the wall.

Leaving the apodyterium, they pass through an arched doorway into the **tepidārium** (warm room) and spend a little time sitting on benches round the wall in a warm, steamy atmosphere, perspiring gently and preparing for the higher temperatures in the next room.

This is the **caldārium** (hot room). At one end of the caldarium there was a large marble bath, rectangular in shape, and stretching across the full width of the room. This bath was filled with hot water in which the bathers sat or wallowed. The Romans did not have soap, but used olive oil instead. After soaking in the bath, Caecilius summons a slave to rub him down with the oil that he has brought with him in a little pot. For this rubbing down, Caecilius lies on a marble slab while the slave works the oil into his skin, and then gently removes it and the dirt with a blunt metal scraper known as a **strigil.** Next comes the masseur to massage skin and muscles. Refreshed by this treatment, Caecilius then goes to the large stone basin at the other end of the caldarium for a rinse down with cold water.

A visit to the baths

These pictures show us a bather's route through the different rooms of the baths after he leaves the palaestra.

They are taken from several different sets of baths, as no one set has all its rooms well preserved today.

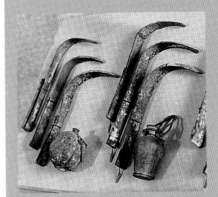

Strigils and oil bottles.

1 *The entrance hall with the apodyterium beyond.* Stabian Baths, Pompeii.

2 *The tepidarium. This sometimes had recesses for clothes like the apodyterium.* Forum Baths, Pompeii.

3 *The hot tub in the caldarium.* Herculaneum.

4 *The caldarium, showing a marble bench for sitting or massage.* Herculaneum.

5 *The frigidarium: cold plunge bath.* Forum Baths, Pompeii.

Before dressing again he might well visit the **frigidārium** (cold room) and there take a plunge in a deep circular pool of unheated water, followed by a brisk rub down with his towel.

Caecilius' visit to the baths was a leisurely social occasion. He enjoyed a noisy, relaxed time in the company of his friends. The Roman writer Seneca lived uncomfortably close to a set of baths in Rome and his description gives us a vivid impression of the atmosphere there:

I am surrounded by uproar. I live over a set of baths. Just imagine the babel of sounds that strikes my ears. When the athletic gentlemen below are exercising themselves, lifting lead weights, I can hear their grunts. I can hear the whistling of their breath as it escapes from their lungs. I can hear somebody enjoying a cheap rub down and the smack of the masseur's hands on his shoulders. If his hand comes down flat, it makes one sound; if it comes down hollowed, it makes another. Add to this the noise of a brawler or thief being arrested down below, the racket made by the man who likes to sing in his bath or the sound of enthusiasts who hurl themselves into the water with a tremendous splash. Next I can hear the screech of the hair-plucker, who advertises himself by shouting. He is never quiet except when he is plucking hair and making his victim shout instead. Finally, just imagine the cries of the cake-seller, the sausage-man, and the other food-sellers as they advertise their goods round the bath, all adding to the din.

A bronze statue of a boxer from a set of baths in Rome. His training would no doubt have contributed to the din about which Seneca complains.

Heating the baths

The Romans were not the first people to build public baths. This was one of the many things they learned from the Greeks. But with their engineering skill the Romans greatly improved the methods of heating them. The previous method had been to heat the water in tanks over a furnace and to stand braziers (portable metal containers in which wood was burnt) in the tepidarium and the caldarium to keep up the air temperature. The braziers were not very efficient and they failed to heat the floor.

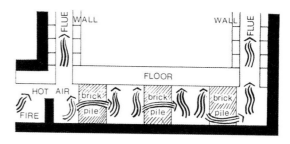

Hypocaust in the Stabian Baths. Notice the floor suspended on brick piles, so that hot air can circulate beneath and warm both the room and the tank of water for bathing.

In the first century BC, a Roman invented the first central heating system. The furnace was placed below the floor level; the floor was supported on small brick piles leaving space through which hot air from the furnace could circulate. In this way, the floor was warmed from below. The hot bath was placed near the furnace and a steady temperature was maintained by the hot air passing immediately below. Later, flues (channels) were built into the walls and warm air from beneath the floor was drawn up through them. This ingenious heating system was known as a **hypocaust.** It was used not only in baths but also in private houses, particularly in the colder parts of the Roman empire. Many examples have been found in Britain. Wood was the fuel most commonly burnt in the furnaces.

Plan of the Forum Baths, Pompeii

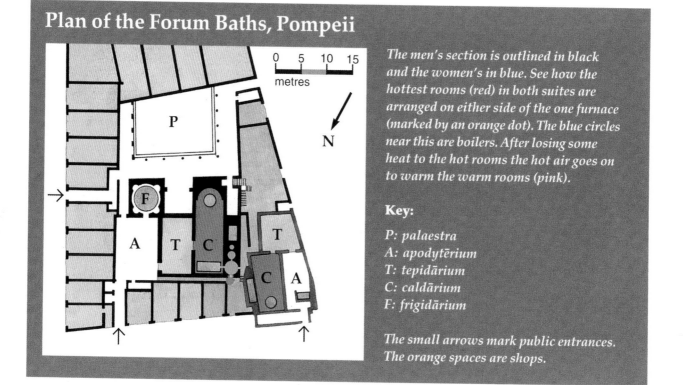

The men's section is outlined in black and the women's in blue. See how the hottest rooms (red) in both suites are arranged on either side of the one furnace (marked by an orange dot). The blue circles near this are boilers. After losing some heat to the hot rooms the hot air goes on to warm the warm rooms (pink).

Key:

P: *palaestra*
A: *apodytērium*
T: *tepidārium*
C: *caldārium*
F: *frigidārium*

The small arrows mark public entrances. The orange spaces are shops.

Vocabulary checklist 9

agnōscit	*recognises*
celeriter	*quickly*
cupit	*wants*
dat	*gives*
diēs	*day*
ēmittit	*throws, sends out*
fert	*brings, carries*
homō	*human being, man*
hospes	*guest*
ille	*that*
īnspicit	*looks at, examines*
iterum	*again*
manet	*remains, stays*
medius	*middle*
mox	*soon*
offert	*offers*
ostendit	*shows*
post	*after*
prōcēdit	*proceeds, advances*
pulcher	*beautiful*
revenit	*comes back, returns*
trādit	*hands over*

The floors of baths often had marine themes. This mosaic of an octopus is in the women's baths at Herculaneum.

RHETOR

STAGE 10

1 Rōmānus dīcit,
   'nōs Rōmānī sumus architectī. nōs viās et pontēs aedificāmus.'

2 'nōs Rōmānī sumus agricolae. nōs fundōs optimōs habēmus.'

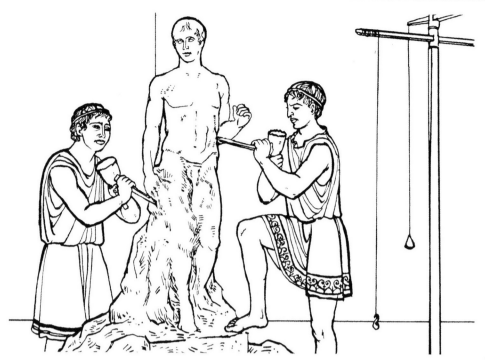

3 Graecus dīcit,
'nōs Graecī sumus sculptōrēs. nōs statuās pulchrās facimus.'

4 'nōs Graecī sumus pictōrēs. nōs pictūrās pingimus.'

5 Rōmānus dīcit,
   'vōs Graecī estis ignāvī. vōs āctōrēs semper spectātis.'

6 Graecus dīcit,
   'vōs Rōmānī estis barbarī. vōs semper pugnātis.'

7 Rōmānus dīcit,
  'nōs sumus callidī. nōs rēs ūtilēs facimus.'

8 Graecus dīcit,
  'nōs sumus callidiōrēs quam vōs. nōs Graecī Rōmānōs docēmus.'

contrōversia

contrōversia *debate*

Quīntus amīcum Graecum habēbat. amīcus erat Alexander.
Quīntus et Alexander ad palaestram ībant, ubi rhētor Graecus
erat. hic rhētor erat Theodōrus et prope palaestram habitābat. in
palaestrā erat porticus longa, ubi Theodōrus iuvenēs docēbat.
postquam ad hanc porticum vēnērunt, Alexander et Quīntus
rhētōrem audīvērunt. rhētor iuvenibus contrōversiam
nūntiābat, 'Graecī sunt meliōrēs quam Rōmānī.'

    Quīntus vehementer exclāmāvit,
    'minimē! nōs Rōmānī sumus meliōrēs quam Graecī.'
    Theodōrus, postquam hanc sententiam audīvit, respondit,
    'haec est tua sententia. nōs tamen nōn sententiam quaerimus,
nōs argūmentum quaerimus.' tum Quīntus rhētōrī et amīcīs
argūmentum explicāvit.

    'nōs Rōmānī sumus fortissimī. nōs barbarōs ferōcissimōs
superāmus. nōs imperium maximum habēmus. nōs pācem
servāmus. vōs Graecī semper contentiōnēs habētis. vōs semper
estis turbulentī.

    nōs sumus architectī optimī. nōs viās et pontēs ubīque
aedificāmus. urbs Rōma est maior quam omnēs urbēs.

    postrēmō nōs Rōmānī dīligenter labōrāmus. deī igitur nōbīs
imperium maximum dant. vōs Graecī estis ignāvī. vōs
numquam labōrātis. deī vōbīs nihil dant.'

5

10

15

20

ībant *were going*
rhētor *teacher*
longa *long*
docēbat *used to teach*
hanc *this*
meliōrēs quam *better than*
minimē! *no!*
sententiam *opinion*
argūmentum *proof*
barbarōs *barbarians*
imperium *empire*
pācem *peace*
servāmus *keep, preserve*
architectī *builders, architects*
pontēs *bridges*
ubīque *everywhere*
aedificāmus *build*
maior quam *greater than, bigger than*
postrēmō *lastly*
deī *gods*
dant *give*
ignāvī *lazy*

postquam Quīntus hanc sententiam explicāvit, iuvenēs
Pompēiānī vehementer plausērunt et eum laudāvērunt. deinde
Alexander surrēxit. iuvenēs Pompēiānī tacuērunt et
Alexandrum intentē spectāvērunt.

'vōs Rōmānī estis miserandī. vōs imperium maximum
habētis, sed vōs estis imitātōrēs; nōs Graecī sumus auctōrēs. vōs
Graecās statuās spectātis, vōs Graecōs librōs legitis, Graecōs
rhētōrēs audītis. vōs Rōmānī estis rīdiculī, quod estis Graeciōrēs
quam nōs Graecī!'

iuvenēs, postquam Alexander sententiam suam explicāvit,
rīsērunt. tum Theodōrus nūntiāvit,
'Alexander victor est. argūmentum optimum explicāvit.'

	deinde *then*
25	**surrēxit** *got up*
	miserandī *pathetic, pitiful*
	imitātōrēs *imitators*
	auctōrēs *creators*
	librōs *books*
30	**legitis** *read*
	rīsērunt *laughed*

Above: *The Romans built this bridge at Alcantara in Spain.*

Greek writers and thinkers have influenced people's minds to this day; far left: the tragic dramatist Euripides; left: the philosopher Anaximander who taught that the universe was governed by law. He is holding a sun-dial, which he is said to have invented.

About the language 1

1   In this Stage, you have met sentences with 'we' and 'you':

nōs labōrāmus.	*We work.*	vōs labōrātis.	*You work.*
nōs currimus.	*We run.*	vōs curritis.	*You run.*

Notice that **vōs labōrātis** and **vōs curritis** are **plural** forms.
They are used when 'you' refers to more than one person.

2   You have now met the whole of the present tense:

(ego)	portō	*I carry, I am carrying*
(tū)	portās	*you (singular) carry, you are carrying*
	portat	*s/he carries, s/he is carrying*
(nōs)	portāmus	*we carry, we are carrying*
(vōs)	portātis	*you (plural) carry, you are carrying*
	portant	*they carry, they are carrying*

3   Notice that **nōs** and **vōs** are not strictly necessary, since the endings
-mus and **-tis** make it clear that 'we' and 'you' are being spoken about.
The Romans generally used **nōs** and **vōs** only for emphasis.

4   Further examples:

   a nōs pugnāmus. vōs dormītis.
   b vōs clāmātis. nōs audīmus.
   c ambulāmus. dīcimus. vidēmus.
   d vidētis. nūntiātis. intrāmus.

5   The Latin for 'we are' and 'you (plural) are' is as follows:

nōs sumus iuvenēs.	*We are young men.*	**vōs estis** pictōrēs.	*You are painters.*
nōs sumus fortēs.	*We are brave.*	**vōs estis** ignāvī.	*You are lazy.*

So the complete present tense of **sum** is:

(ego)	sum	*I am*
(tū)	es	*you (singular) are*
	est	*s/he is*
(nōs)	sumus	*we are*
(vōs)	estis	*you (plural) are*
	sunt	*they are*

statuae

postquam Theodōrus Alexandrum laudāvit, iuvenēs Pompēiānī ē porticū discessērunt. Alexander et Quīntus ad vīllam ambulābant, ubi Alexander et duo frātrēs habitābant.

Alexander frātribus dōnum quaerēbat, quod diem nātālem celebrābant.

in viā īnstitor parvās statuās vēndēbat et clāmābat:

'statuae! optimae statuae!'

Alexander frātribus statuās ēmit. statuae erant senex, iuvenis, puella pulchra. Alexander, postquam statuās ēmit, ad vīllam cum Quīntō contendit.

duo frātrēs in hortō sedēbant. Diodōrus pictūram pingēbat, Thrasymachus librum Graecum legēbat. postquam Alexander et Quīntus vīllam intrāvērunt, puerī ad eōs cucurrērunt. Diodōrus statuās cōnspexit.

'Alexander, quid portās?' inquit.

'vōs estis fēlīcēs', inquit Alexander. 'ego vōbīs dōnum habeō quod vōs diem nātālem celebrātis. ecce!' Alexander frātribus statuās ostendit.

'quam pulchra est puella!' inquit Diodōrus. 'dā mihi puellam!'

'minimē! frāter, dā mihi puellam!' clāmāvit Thrasymachus. puerī dissentiēbant et lacrimābant.

'hercle! vōs estis stultissimī puerī!' clāmāvit Alexander īrātus. 'semper dissentītis, semper lacrimātis. abīte! abīte! ego statuās retineō!'

puerī, postquam Alexander hoc dīxit, abiērunt. Diodōrus pictūram in terram dēiēcit, quod īrātus erat. Thrasymachus librum in piscīnam dēiēcit, quod īrātissimus erat.

tum Quīntus dīxit,

'Alexander, dā mihi statuās! Thrasymache! Diodōre! venīte hūc! Thrasymache, ecce! ego tibi senem dō, quod senex erat philosophus. Diodōre, tibi iuvenem dō, quod iuvenis erat pictor. ego mihi puellam dō, quod ego sum sōlus! vōsne estis contentī?'

'sumus contentī', respondērunt puerī.

'ecce, Alexander', inquit Quīntus, 'vōs Graeculī estis optimī artificēs sed turbulentī. nōs Rōmānī vōbīs pācem damus.'

'et vōs praemium accipitis', susurrāvit Thrasymachus.

frātrēs *brothers*

īnstitor *pedlar, street vendor*

10 ad eōs *to them*
fēlīcēs *lucky*
quam! *how!*
dā! *give!*
dissentiēbant *were arguing*
15 stultissimī *very stupid*
abīte! *go away!*
retineō *am keeping*
abiērunt *went away*
in terram *onto the ground*
20 dēiēcit *threw*
in piscīnam *into the fish-pond*
venīte hūc! *come here!*
philosophus *philosopher*
sōlus *lonely*
25 vōsne estis contentī? *are you satisfied?*
Graeculī *poor Greeks*
artificēs *artists*
praemium *profit, reward*
30 susurrāvit *whispered, muttered*

statuae.

About the language 2

1   Study the following pairs of sentences:

> nōs Rōmānī sumus callidī.
> *We Romans are clever.*

> nōs Rōmānī sumus **callidiōrēs** quam vōs Graecī.
> *We Romans are **cleverer** than you Greeks.*

> nōs Rōmānī sumus fortēs.
> *We Romans are brave.*

> nōs Rōmānī sumus **fortiōrēs** quam vōs Graecī.
> *We Romans are **braver** than you Greeks.*

The words in **bold type** are known as **comparatives**. They are used to compare two things or groups with each other. In the examples above, the Romans are comparing themselves with the Greeks.

2   Further examples:

a   Pompēiānī sunt stultī. Nūcerīnī sunt stultiōrēs quam Pompēiānī.
b   Diodōrus erat īrātus, sed Thrasymachus erat īrātior quam Diodōrus.
c   mea vīlla est pulchra, sed tua vīlla est pulchrior quam mea.

3   The word **magnus** forms its comparative in an unusual way:

> Nūceria est magna.   Rōma est maior quam Nūceria.
> *Nuceria is large.*   *Rome is larger than Nuceria.*

ānulus Aegyptius

Aegyptius *Egyptian*

When you have read this story, answer the questions at the end.

Syphāx in tabernā sedēbat. caupō Syphācī vīnum dedit. Syphāx caupōnī ānulum trādidit.

'pecūniam nōn habeō', inquit, 'quod Neptūnus nāvem meam dēlēvit.'

caupō, postquam ānulum accēpit, eum īnspexit.

'ānulus antīquus est', inquit.

'ita vērō, antīquus est', Syphāx caupōnī respondit. 'servus

caupō *innkeeper*

Neptūnus *Neptune (god of
the sea)*

5   **dēlēvit** *has destroyed*
antīquus *old, ancient*

Aegyptius mihi ānulum dedit. servus in pȳramide ānulum invēnit.'

    caupō, postquam tabernam clausit, ad vīllam suam festīnāvit. 10
caupō uxōrī ānulum ostendit. caupō uxōrī ānulum dedit, quod
ānulus eam dēlectāvit.

    uxor postrīdiē ad urbem contendēbat. subitō servus ingēns in
viā appāruit. pecūniam postulāvit. fēmina, quod erat perterrita,
servō pecūniam dedit. servus ānulum cōnspexit. ānulum 15
postulāvit. fēmina servō eum trādidit.

    fēmina ad tabernam rediit et marītum quaesīvit. mox eum
invēnit. caupō incendium spectābat. ēheu! taberna ardēbat!
fēmina marītō rem tōtam nārrāvit.

    'ānulus īnfēlīx est', inquit caupō. 'ānulus tabernam meam 20
dēlēvit.'

    servus ingēns, postquam pecūniam et ānulum cēpit, ad
urbem contendit. subitō trēs servōs cōnspexit. servī inimīcī
erant. inimīcī, postquam pecūniam cōnspexērunt, servum
verberābant. servus fūgit, sed ānulum āmīsit. 25

    Grumiō cum Poppaeā ambulābat. ānulum in viā invēnit.
    'quid vidēs?' rogāvit Poppaea.
    'ānulum videō', inquit. 'ānulus Aegyptius est.'
    'euge!' inquit Poppaea. 'ānulus fēlīx est.'

in pȳramide *in a pyramid*

clausit *shut*

eam *her*
postrīdiē *on the next day*

marītum *husband*
incendium *blaze, fire*
ardēbat *was on fire*
īnfēlīx *unlucky*

cēpit *took*

āmīsit *lost*

Questions

        Marks

1 How did Syphax pay for his drink?   1
2 Why did he pay in this way?   1
3 What do you think he meant in lines 3 and 4 by saying **Neptūnus
    nāvem meam dēlēvit**?   2
4 In lines 7–9, Syphax gives three pieces of information about
    the ring. What are they?   3
5 What did the innkeeper do with the ring when he returned home?   2
6 **uxor postrīdiē ad urbem contendēbat** (line 13). Who met the wife?
    What two things did he make her do?   1 + 2
7 What did she find when she returned to the inn (line 18)?   1
8 What three things happened after the huge slave met the other
    slaves and they spotted the money (lines 24-5)?   3
9 Who found the ring?   1
10 Poppaea thought the ring was lucky. Who had the opposite
    opinion earlier in the story? Who do you think was right?
    Give a reason.   1 + 2

        TOTAL **20**

Practising the language

1   Complete each sentence with the most suitable phrase from the box below.
    Then translate the sentence.

    a   nōs sumus rhētōrēs Graecī; nōs in palaestrā . . . .
    b   nōs sumus āctōrēs nōtissimī; nōs in theātrō . . . .
    c   nōs sumus ancillae pulchrae; nōs fēminīs . . . .
    d   nōs sumus coquī; nōs dominīs . . . .
    e   nōs sumus pistōrēs; nōs cīvibus . . . .

fābulam agimus
contrōversiam habēmus
cibum offerimus
stolās compōnimus
pānem parāmus

2   Complete each sentence with the most suitable noun from the box below.
    Then translate the sentence.

    a   vōs estis . . . . . . callidī; vōs pictūrās magnificās pingitis.
    b   vōs estis . . . . . . fortēs; vōs in arēnā pugnātis.
    c   nōs sumus . . . . . . ; nōs in thermīs togās custōdīmus.
    d   vōs servōs in forō vēnditis, quod vōs estis . . . .
    e   nōs ad palaestram contendimus, quod nōs sumus . . . .

servī	āthlētae
pictōrēs	vēnālīciī
gladiātōrēs	

Schools

The first stage of education

Quintus would have first gone to school when he was about
seven years old. Like other Roman schools, the one that Quintus
attended would have been small and consisted of about thirty
pupils and a teacher known as the **lūdī magister.** All the
teaching would take place in a rented room or perhaps in a
public colonnade or square, where there would be constant
noise and distractions.

Parents were not obliged by law to send their children to
school, and those who wanted education for their children had
to pay for it. The charges were not high and the advantages of
being able to read and write were so widely appreciated that
many people were prepared to pay for their sons to go to school
at least for a few years.

Sometimes girls were sent to school too, but generally they
would stay at home and pick up a knowledge of reading and
writing from their parents or brothers. Most of their time would

be spent learning the skills of a good housewife: cooking, cleaning, childcare and perhaps spinning and weaving. Girls from wealthy families would have to be trained to organise a household of slaves. By the time they were fourteen they were usually married.

On the journey between home and school, pupils were normally escorted by a slave known as a **paedagōgus** who was responsible for their behaviour and protection. Another slave carried their books and writing materials.

At the school of the ludi magister Quintus would have learnt only to read and write Latin and Greek and perhaps to do some simple arithmetic. Like most Roman boys he would already be able to speak some Greek, which he would have picked up from Greek slaves at home or friends like Alexander in the story.

tabulae and stili.

Writing materials

The materials that Quintus used for writing were rather different from ours. Frequently he wrote on **tabulae** (wooden tablets) coated with a thin film of wax; and he inscribed the letters on the wax surface with a thin stick of metal, bone or ivory. This stick was called a **stilus.** The end opposite the writing point was flat so that it could be used to rub out mistakes and make the wax smooth again. Several tablets were strung together to make a little writing-book. At other times he wrote with ink on papyrus, a material that looked rather like modern paper but was rougher in texture. It was manufactured from the fibres of the papyrus reed that grew along the banks of the River Nile in Egypt. For writing on papyrus he used either a reed or a goose-quill sharpened and split at one end like the modern pen-nib. Ink was made from soot and resin or other gummy substances, forming a paste that was thinned by adding water.

Papyrus rolls, a double inkwell (for red and black ink) and a quill pen. From a Pompeian painting.

A wax tablet with a schoolboy's exercise in Greek. The master has written the top two lines and the child has copied them below.

The best inks were so hard and durable that they are perfectly legible even today on the pieces of papyrus that have survived.

Pictures of scenes in school show that there were generally no desks and no blackboard. Pupils sat on benches or stools, resting tablets on their knees. The master sat on a high chair overlooking his class. Discipline was usually strict and sometimes harsh.

The school-day began early and lasted for six hours with a short break at midday. Holidays were given on public festivals and on every ninth day which was a market-day; during the hot summer months fewer pupils attended lessons, and some schoolmasters may have closed their schools altogether from July to October.

Two boys and their teacher at school. The boys are using papyrus rolls.

The second stage

Many children would have finished their schooling at the age of eleven, but a boy like Quintus, from a wealthy family, would have moved to a more advanced school run by a **grammaticus.** The grammaticus introduced his pupils to the work of famous Greek and Roman writers, beginning with the *Iliad* and *Odyssey* of Homer. Then the pupils moved on to the famous Greek tragedies which had been first performed in Athens in the fifth century BC. The Roman poets most frequently read at schools were Virgil and Horace. Besides reading works of literature aloud, the pupils had to analyse the grammar and learn long passages by heart; many educated people could remember these passages in later life and quote or recite them. The pupils were also taught a little history and geography, mainly in order to understand references to famous people and places mentioned in the literature.

When he left the grammaticus at the age of fifteen or sixteen, Quintus would have a very good knowledge of Greek as well as Latin. This knowledge of Greek not only introduced the pupils to a culture which the Romans greatly admired and which had inspired much of their own civilisation, but was also very useful in later life because Greek was widely spoken in the countries of the eastern Mediterranean where Roman merchants and government officials frequently travelled on business.

This roughly sketched painting shows a school in session in the colonnade of the forum at Pompeii. On the right a boy is supported on another's back, for a beating.

The third stage

A few students then proceeded to the school of a **rhētor,** like Theodorus in our story. This teacher, who was often a highly educated Greek, gave more advanced lessons in literature and trained his students in the art of public speaking. This was a very important skill for young men who expected to take part in public life. For example, they needed it to present cases in the law courts, to express their opinions in council meetings, and to address the people at election time. The rhetor taught the rules for making different kinds of speeches and made his students practise arguing for and against a point of view. Students also learned how to vary their tone of voice and emphasise their words with gestures.

Science and technical subjects

We have not so far mentioned the teaching of science and technical subjects in Roman schools. It is true that the Greeks had made important discoveries in mathematics and some aspects of physics; it is also true that the Romans were experienced in such things as the methods of surveying and the use of concrete in building. But these things played little part in school work. The purpose of ordinary Roman schools was to teach those things which were thought to be most necessary for civilised living: the ability to read and write, a knowledge of simple arithmetic, the appreciation of fine literature and the ability to speak and argue convincingly. Science and advanced mathematics were taught to only a few students whose parents were interested and wealthy enough to pay the fees of a specialist teacher, nearly always a Greek. Technical skills were learnt by becoming an apprentice in a trade or business.

The poet Virgil.

Craft skills were learned by apprenticeship. Here: carving a table leg.

Vocabulary checklist 10

abit	goes away
accipit	accepts
callidus	clever, cunning
contentus	satisfied
exclāmat	exclaims
frāter	brother
habitat	lives
imperium	empire
invenit	finds
liber	book
nōs	we
nūntiat	announces
pāx	peace
portus	harbour
quam	than
semper	always
servat	saves, looks after
sōlus	alone
suus	his, her, their
tacet	is silent, is quiet
uxor	wife
vehementer	violently, loudly
vōs	you (plural)

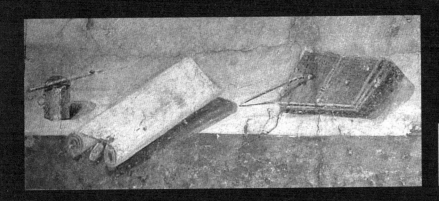

A pen (made from a reed), inkwell, papyrus roll, stilus and wax tablets.

CANDIDATI

STAGE 11

1 cīvēs in forō candidātōs spectant.

2 agricolae clāmant,
   'nōs candidātum optimum habēmus.'
   'candidātus noster est Lūcius.'
   'nōs Lūciō favēmus.'

3 mercātōrēs agricolīs respondent,
   'nōs candidātum optimum habēmus.'
   'candidātus noster est mercātor.'
   'nōs mercātōrī favēmus.'

4 pistōrēs in forō clāmant,
  'nōs pistōrēs candidātum optimum
  habēmus.'
  'candidātus noster est pistor.'
  'nōs pistōrī crēdimus.'

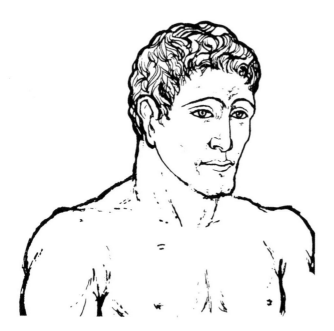

5 iuvenēs pistōribus respondent,
  'nōs iuvenēs candidātum optimum
  habēmus.'
  'candidātus noster est āthlēta.'
  'nōs āthlētae crēdimus.'

6 fūrēs clāmant,
  'nōs quoque candidātum habēmus.'
  'candidātus noster est fūr.'
  'nōs candidātō nostrō nōn crēdimus sed
  favēmus.'

Marcus et Quārtus

Marcus Tullius et Quārtus Tullius erant frātrēs. Marcus et Quārtus in vīllā contentiōnem habēbant. Marcus Quārtō dīxit,

'Āfer candidātus optimus est. Āfer multās vīllās et multās tabernās habet. Pompēiānī Āfrō favent, quod vir dīves est.'

'minimē! Holcōnius candidātus optimus est', Quārtus frātrī respondit. 'Holcōnius est vir nōbilis. Pompēiānī Holcōniō crēdunt, quod pater senātor erat.'

Quārtus, quod erat īrātissimus, ē vīllā discessit. Quārtus sibi dīxit,

'frāter meus est stultissimus. gēns nostra Holcōniō semper favet.'

Quārtus per viam ambulābat et rem cōgitābat. subitō parvam tabernam cōnspexit, ubi scrīptor habitābat. scrīptor Sulla erat. Quārtus, postquam tabernam vīdit, cōnsilium cēpit. tabernam intrāvit et Sullam ad vīllam suam invītāvit.

postquam ad vīllam vēnērunt, Quārtus Sullae mūrum ostendit.

'scrībe hunc titulum!' inquit. 'scrībe "Quārtus et frāter Holcōniō favent. Quārtus et frāter Holcōniō crēdunt".'

Quārtus scrīptōrī decem dēnāriōs dedit.

'placetne tibi?' rogāvit Quārtus.

'mihi placet', Sulla Quārtō respondit. Sulla, postquam dēnāriōs accēpit, titulum in mūrō scrīpsit.

candidātus *candidate*
favent *favour, give support to*
5 **vir dīves** *a rich man*
vir nōbilis *a man of noble birth*
crēdunt *trust, have faith in*

sibi dīxit *said to himself*
10 **gēns nostra** *our family*
rem cōgitābat *was considering the problem*
scrīptor *sign-writer*
cōnsilium cēpit *had an idea*
15
mūrum *wall*

scrībe! *write!*
titulum *notice, slogan*
20
placetne tibi? *does it please you? does it suit you?*
scrīpsit *wrote*

Sulla

Marcus ē vīllā vēnit. Sullam vīdit. titulum cōnspexit. postquam
titulum lēgit, īrātus erat. Marcus scrīptōrem valdē vituperāvit.

'frāter tuus mē ad vīllam invītāvit', inquit Sulla. 'frāter tuus
mihi decem dēnāriōs dedit.'

'frāter meus est stultior quam asinus', Marcus Sullae
respondit. 'in vīllā nostrā ego sum dominus, quod sum senior.
Sulla, ērāde illam īnscrīptiōnem! scrībe titulum novum!'

Marcus Sullae quīndecim dēnāriōs dedit.

'placetne tibi?' rogāvit.

'mihi placet', Sulla Marcō respondit. Sulla, postquam
īnscrīptiōnem ērāsit, hunc titulum scrīpsit, 'Marcus et frāter Āfrō
favent. Marcus et frāter Āfrō crēdunt.'

Marcus erat laetissimus et frātrem ē vīllā vocāvit. Marcus
frātrī titulum novum ostendit. Quārtus, postquam titulum lēgit,
īrātus erat. Quārtus Marcum pulsāvit. tum frātrēs in viā
pugnābant!

'Marce! Quārte! dēsistite! intrō īte!' clāmāvit Sulla. 'cōnsilium
optimum habeō.'

postquam frātrēs vīllam intrāvērunt, Sulla celeriter rem
cōnfēcit.

duōs titulōs in mūrō scrīpsit. tum frātrēs ē vīllā vocāvit.

scrīptor frātribus mūrum ostendit. ecce! Marcus hunc titulum
vīdit: 'Marcus Āfrō favet. Āfer est candidātus optimus.'

'euge! hic titulus mē valdē dēlectat', inquit Marcus.
Quārtus alterum titulum in mūrō cōnspexit:
'Quārtus Holcōniō favet. Holcōnius est candidātus optimus.'
Quārtus quoque laetissimus erat.

frātrēs Sullae trīgintā dēnāriōs dedērunt. Sulla rīdēbat.
postquam Marcus et Quārtus discessērunt, tertium titulum
addidit:

5   **asinus** *ass, donkey*
   senior *the elder*
   ērāde! *rub out! erase!*
   īnscrīptiōnem *writing*

10

   ērāsit *rubbed out, erased*

15

   dēsistite! *stop!*
   intrō īte! *go inside!*
20   **rem cōnfēcit** *finished the job*

25

30   **tertium** *third*
   addidit *added*
   līberālissimī *very generous*

MARCVS ET QVARTVS
SVNT LIBERALISSIMI

About the language 1

1 In Stage 9, you met the dative case:

> mercātor **Metellae** togam trādidit.
> *The merchant handed over the toga **to Metella**.*

> Grumiō **hospitibus** cēnam parābat.
> *Grumio was preparing a meal **for the guests**.*

2 In Stage 11, you have met some further examples:

> Quārtus **Holcōniō** favet. nōs **pistōrī** crēdimus.
> *Quartus gives support **to Holconius**.* *We give our trust **to the baker**.*

3 The sentences above can be translated more simply:

> Quārtus Holcōniō favet. nōs pistōrī crēdimus.
> *Quartus supports Holconius.* *We trust the baker.*

4 Further examples:

a nōs Āfrō favēmus.
b vōs amīcīs crēditis.
c mercātōrēs candidātō nostrō nōn crēdunt.

5 Notice the following use of the dative with the verb **placet:**

> placetne tibi? mihi placet.
> *Is it pleasing to you?* *It is pleasing to me.*

There are more natural ways of translating these examples, such as:

> *Does it please you?* *Yes, it pleases me.*
> *Do you like it?* *Yes, I do.*

6 Notice the dative of **nōs** and **vōs:**

> nōs sumus fortēs. deī **nōbīs** imperium dant.
> *We are brave. The gods give an empire **to us**.*

> vōs estis ignāvī. deī **vōbīs** nihil dant.
> *You are lazy. The gods give nothing **to you**.*

Lūcius Spurius Pompōniānus

in vīllā

Grumiō ē culīnā contendit. Clēmēns Grumiōnem videt.

Clēmēns:	babae! togam splendidam geris!	**babae!** *hey!*
Grumiō:	placetne tibi?	
Clēmēns:	mihi placet. quō festīnās, Grumiō?	**quō?** *where?*
Grumiō:	ad amphitheātrum contendō. Āfer fautōrēs exspectat.	5 **fautōrēs** *supporters*
Clēmēns:	num tū Āfrō favēs? Caecilius Holcōniō favet.	
Grumiō:	Āfer fautōribus quīnque dēnāriōs prōmīsit. Holcōnius fautōribus duōs dēnāriōs tantum prōmīsit. ego Āfrō faveō, quod vir līberālis est.	**quīnque** *five* **prōmīsit** *promised* 10 **tantum** *only*
Clēmēns:	sed tū servus es. cīvis Pompēiānus nōn es. Āfer cīvibus Pompēiānīs pecūniam prōmīsit.	
Grumiō:	Clēmēns, hodiē nōn sum Grumiō. hodiē sum Lūcius Spurius Pompōniānus!	
Clēmēns:	Lūcius Spurius Pompōniānus! mendācissimus coquus es!	15 **mendācissimus** *very deceitful*
Grumiō:	minimē! hodiē sum pistor Pompēiānus. hodiē nōs pistōrēs ad amphitheātrum convenīmus. nōs Āfrum ad forum dūcimus, ubi cīvēs ōrātiōnēs exspectant. ego ad amphitheātrum contendō. tū mēcum venīs?	**ad amphitheātrum** *at the amphitheatre* 20 **convenīmus** *gather, meet* **ōrātiōnēs** *speeches* **mēcum** *with me*
Clēmēns:	tēcum veniō. Āfrō nōn faveō. dēnāriōs nōn cupiō, sed dē tē sollicitus sum. rem perīculōsam suscipis. *(exeunt.)*	**dē tē** *about you* **perīculōsam** *dangerous* **suscipis** *you are taking on* **exeunt** *they go out*

prope amphitheātrum

multī pistōrēs ad amphitheātrum conveniunt. Grumiō et Clēmēns ad
hanc turbam festīnant.

dīvīsor:	festīnāte! festīnāte! nōs Āfrum exspectāmus.	
Grumiō:	salvē, dīvīsor! ego sum Lūcius Spurius Pompōniānus	
	et hic *(Grumiō Clēmentem pulsat)* servus meus est.	5
	ego et Āfer amīcissimī sumus.	
dīvīsor:	ecce quīnque dēnāriī!	
	(dīvīsor Grumiōnī dēnāriōs dat. dīvīsor Grumiōnī	
	fūstem quoque trādit.)	
Grumiō:	Āfer mihi dēnāriōs, nōn fūstem prōmīsit.	10
Clēmēns:	Āfer vir līberālis est.	
Grumiō:	tacē, pessime serve!	
dīvīsor:	fūstēs ūtilissimī sunt. Holcōnius et amīcī sunt in forō.	
pistor:	ecce Āfer! Āfer adest!	
	(Āfer et fautōrēs per viās ad forum contendunt.)	15

dīvīsor *agent (hired to*
distribute bribes at elections)
festīnāte! *hurry!*
amīcissimī *very friendly, very*
good friends

tacē! *shut up! be quiet!*
ūtilissimī *very useful*

in forō

pistōrēs cum Clēmente et cum Grumiōne Āfrum ad forum dūcunt.

pistor prīmus:	Pompēiānī Āfrō favent.	
pistor secundus:	Āfer est melior quam Holcōnius.	
pistor tertius:	nōs Āfrō crēdimus.	
Clēmēns:	Grumiō! in forō sunt Holcōnius et amīcī.	5
	Holcōnium et amīcōs videō.	
Grumiō:	euge! fēminās videō, ancillās videō,	
	puellās… ēheu! Caecilium videō! Caecilius	
	cum Holcōniō stat! ad vīllam reveniō!	
Clēmēns:	Grumiō, manē!	10
	(Grumiō fugit.)	
mercātor prīmus:	Holcōnius est vir nōbilis.	
mercātor secundus:	Holcōnius melior est quam Āfer.	
mercātor tertius:	nōs mercātōrēs Holcōniō favēmus.	
	(pistōrēs et mercātōrēs conveniunt. īrātī sunt.)	15
pistor prīmus:	Holcōnius est asinus. vōs quoque estis	
	asinī, quod Holcōniō crēditis.	
mercātor prīmus:	Āfer est caudex. vōs quoque estis caudicēs,	
	quod Āfrō crēditis.	
pistor secundus:	amīcī! mercātōrēs nōs 'caudicēs' vocant.	20
	nōs nōn sumus caudicēs. fortissimī sumus.	
	fūstēs habēmus.	

caudex *blockhead, idiot*

mercātor secundus:	amīcī! pistōrēs nōs 'asinōs' vocant. nōs nōn sumus asinī. nōs fortiōrēs sumus quam pistōrēs. magnōs fūstēs habēmus. *(mercātōrēs et pistōrēs in forō pugnant.)*

25

in culīnā

Clēmēns in culīnā sedet. Grumiō intrat.

Clēmēns:	salvē, Pompōniāne! hercle! toga tua scissa est!	**scissa** *torn*
Grumiō:	ēheu! Holcōnius et amīcī in forō mē cēpērunt. postquam fūstem meum cōnspexērunt, clāmābant, 'ecce pistor fortis!' tum mercātōrēs mē 5 verberāvērunt. dēnāriōs meōs rapuērunt. nunc nūllōs dēnāriōs habeō.	**rapuērunt** *seized, grabbed*
Clēmēns:	ego decem dēnāriōs habeō!	
Grumiō:	decem dēnāriōs?	
Clēmēns:	Caecilius mihi decem dēnāriōs dedit, quod servus 10 fidēlis sum. postquam pistōrēs et mercātōrēs pugnam commīsērunt, Caecilius mē cōnspexit. duo pistōrēs Caecilium verberābant. dominus noster auxilium postulābat. Caecilius mēcum ē forō effūgit. dominus noster mihi decem dēnāriōs dedit, quod 15 līberālis est.	**auxilium** *help* **effūgit** *escaped*
Grumiō:	Caecilius est …	
Clēmēns:	valē, Pompōniāne!	
Grumiō:	quō festīnās, Clēmēns?	
Clēmēns:	ad portum festīnō. ibi Poppaea mē exspectat. placetne tibi?	20 **ibi** *there*
Grumiō:	mihi nōn placet!	

Right: *Pompeians listening to a candidate speaking from the steps of the temple of Jupiter.*

Above: *Candidates also made speeches from a special platform in the forum.*

About the language 2

1   So far you have met the following ways of asking questions in Latin:

- By tone of voice, indicated in writing by a question mark:

    tū pecūniam dēbēs?   *Do you owe money?*
    tū ānulum habēs?   *Do you have the ring?*

- By means of a question word such as **quis, quid, ubi, cūr:**

    quis est Quīntus?   *Who is Quintus?*
    quid tū facis?   *What are you doing?*
    ubi est ānulus?   *Where is the ring?*
    cūr tū lacrimās?   *Why are you crying?*

- By adding **-ne** to the first word of the sentence:

    vōsne estis contentī? *Are you satisfied?*
    placetne tibi?   *Does it please you?*

2   Further examples:

   a   cūr tū in hortō labōrās?
   b   quis est āthlēta ille?
   c   tū discum habēs?
   d   vōsne estis īrātī?
   e   ubi sunt mercātōrēs?
   f   quid quaeris, domina?
   g   tūne Pompēiānus es?
   h   quis vīnum portat?
   i   cēnam parās?
   j   ubi sumus?

Practising the language

1 Complete each sentence with the right form of the verb from the box below. Then translate the sentence. Do not use any word more than once.

contendō	faveō
contendis	favēs
contendimus	favēmus
contenditis	favētis

a ego ad forum . . . . ego sum candidātus.
b tū Āfrō . . . . tū es stultus.
c ego Holcōniō . . . ., quod Holcōnius est candidātus optimus.
d nōs Holcōniō nōn . . . ., quod Holcōnius est asinus.
e Clēmēns, cūr tū ad portum . . . . ?
f vōs Āfrō . . . ., quod vōs estis pistōrēs.
g nōs ad vīllam . . . ., quod in forō sunt Holcōnius et amīcī.
h ēheu! cūr ē forō . . . . ? vōs dēnāriōs meōs habētis!

2 Complete each sentence with the right form of the noun. Then translate the sentence.

a Quārtus Sullae decem dēnāriōs dedit. Sulla . . . . in mūrō scrīpsit. (titulus, titulum)
b fūr thermās intrābat. . . . . eum agnōvit. (mercātor, mercātōrem)
c multī candidātī sunt in forō. ego . . . . videō. (Holcōnius, Holcōnium)
d ego ad portum currō. . . . . mē exspectat. (ancilla, ancillae)
e hodiē ad urbem contendō. in amphitheātrō sunt. . . . . (leō, leōnēs)
f rhētor est īrātus. rhētor . . . . exspectat. (puerī, puerōs)
g fēminae sunt in tabernā. mercātōrēs fēminīs . . . . ostendunt. (stolae, stolās)
h postquam Holcōnius et amīcī Grumiōnem cēpērunt, quīnque . . . . rapuērunt. (dēnāriī, dēnāriōs)

Local government and elections

The Pompeians took local politics seriously, and the annual elections, which were held at the end of March, were very lively. As soon as the names of candidates were published, election fever gripped the town. Slogans appeared on the walls, groups of supporters held processions through the streets and the candidates spoke at public meetings in the forum.

The meeting place of the town council.

Every year, two pairs of officials were elected by the people. The senior pair, called **duovirī,** were responsible for hearing evidence and giving judgement in the law court. The other pair, called **aedīlēs,** had the task of supervising the public markets, the police force, the baths, places of public entertainment, the water supply and sewers. It was their duty to see that the public services were efficiently run and the local taxes spent wisely.

In addition to these four officials, there was a town council of one hundred leading citizens, most of whom had already served as duoviri or aediles. New members were chosen not by the people but by the council itself.

The candidates wore a toga, specially whitened with chalk, in order to be easily recognised. The word **candidātus** is connected with **candidus** which means 'dazzling white'. As they walked around attended by their clients and greeting voters, their agents praised their qualities, made promises on their behalf, and distributed bribes in the form of money. This financial bribery was illegal but was widely practised. Legal forms of persuasion included promises of games and entertainments if the candidate won. In fact, it was expected that those who were elected would show their gratitude to the voters by putting on splendid shows in the theatre and amphitheatre at their own expense.

A successful candidate would also be expected to contribute from his own wealth to the construction or repair of public buildings. The family of the Holconii, whose names often appear in the lists of Pompeian duoviri and aediles, were connected with the building of the large theatre, and another wealthy family, the Flacci, helped to pay for other civic buildings. The Flacci also had a reputation for putting on first-class entertainments.

The public officials might provide free bread for the poor. One election slogan recommends a candidate who 'brings good bread'.

This tradition of public service was encouraged by the emperors and was an important part of Roman public life. It made it possible for a small town like Pompeii to enjoy benefits which could not have been paid for by local taxes alone. It also meant that men who wanted to take part in the government of their town had to be wealthy. They came from two groups: a small core of wealthy families, like the Holconii, whose members were regularly elected to the most important offices, and a larger, less powerful group which changed frequently.

Although public service was unpaid and was not a means of making money, it gave a man a position of importance in his town. The wide seats in the front row of the theatre, which gave a close-up view of the chorus and actors, were reserved for him; he also had a special place close to the arena in the amphitheatre. In due course the town council might erect a statue to him and he would have his name inscribed on any building to whose construction or repair he had contributed. The Romans were not modest people. They were eager for honour and fame amongst their fellow citizens. There was therefore no shortage of candidates to compete for these rewards at election time.

Caecilius does not seem to have stood as a candidate, although in many ways he was an outstanding citizen and had made a considerable fortune. Perhaps he preferred to concentrate on his business activities and was content to support candidates from the great political families like the Holconii.

Pompeii was free to run its own affairs. But if the local officials were unable to preserve law and order, the central government at Rome might take over and run the town. This actually happened after the famous riot in AD 59 described in Stage 8, when the people of nearby Nuceria quarrelled with the Pompeians at a gladiatorial show given by Livineius Regulus, and many were killed or wounded. The Nucerians complained to the Emperor Nero; Regulus himself was sent into exile and games in Pompeii were banned for ten years.

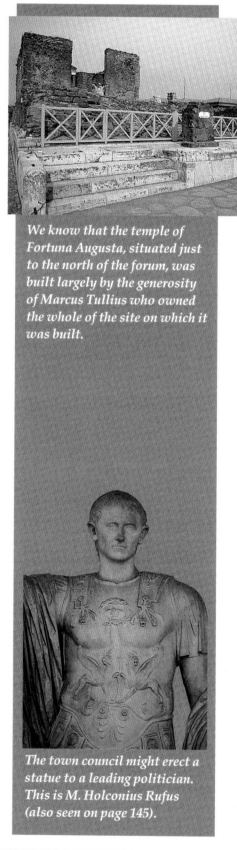

We know that the temple of Fortuna Augusta, situated just to the north of the forum, was built largely by the generosity of Marcus Tullius who owned the whole of the site on which it was built.

The town council might erect a statue to a leading politician. This is M. Holconius Rufus (also seen on page 145).

This notice reads: 'Vote for Cnaeus Helvius Sabinus as aedile. He deserves public office.'

Election notices

Many of the thousands of graffiti found in Pompeii refer to the elections held there in March, AD 79. Here are two of them:

> Casellius for aedile.
>
> We want Tiberius Claudius Verus for duovir.

Political supporters represented all kinds of people and interests. Sometimes they were groups of neighbours who lived in the same area as the candidate. They would certainly include the candidate's personal friends and his clients. Sometimes, however, appeals were made to particular trade groups. One notice reads:

> Innkeepers, vote for Sallustius Capito!

Others are addressed to barbers, mule-drivers, pack-carriers, bakers and fishermen. It is thought that most of the slogans were organised by the agents of the candidates and groups of their supporters rather than by private individuals.

This method of electioneering by wall slogans naturally invited replies by rival supporters. One candidate, Vatia, was made to look ridiculous by this comment:

All the people who are fast asleep vote for Vatia.

Pompeian women did not have the right to vote. Only adult male citizens were allowed to cast votes in the voting hall on election day. Nevertheless, women certainly took a lively interest in local politics and supported the various candidates vigorously. There are, for example, several slogans written by the girls who worked in a bar belonging to a woman called Asellina.

Painting election notices

It appears that these notices were often painted on the walls at night by lantern light. The streets were then more or less deserted, and so there was less risk of trouble from rival supporters. It was also easier at night to put up a ladder for an hour or two without causing congestion on the pavements.

At top right there is part of a notice advertising a fight of ten pairs of gladiators. It may have been paid for by a candidate in the elections.

Vocabulary checklist 11

capit	*takes*
cīvis	*citizen*
convenit	*gathers, meets*
crēdit	*trusts, believes*
dē	*about*
favet	*supports*
invītat	*invites*
it	*goes*
legit	*reads*
līberālis	*generous*
minimē!	*no!*
mūrus	*wall*
noster	*our*
nunc	*now*
placet	*it pleases*
prīmus	*first*
prōmittit	*promises*
pugna	*fight*
senātor	*senator*
sollicitus	*worried, anxious*
stultus	*stupid*
valē!	*goodbye!*
verberat	*strikes, beats*
vir	*man*

L. Ceius Secundus is proposed for aedile.

VESUVIUS

STAGE 12

mōns īrātus

1 Syphāx et Celer in portū stābant. amīcī montem spectābant.

2 Syphāx amīcō dīxit,
  'ego prope portum servōs vēndēbam.
  ego subitō sonōs audīvī.'

3 Celer Syphācī respondit,
  'tū sonōs audīvistī. ego tremōrēs sēnsī.
  ego prope montem ambulābam.'

4 Poppaea et Lucriō in ātriō stābant.
sollicitī erant.

5 Poppaea Lucriōnī dīxit,
'ego in forō eram. ego tibi togam quaerēbam.
ego nūbem mīrābilem cōnspexī.'

6 Lucriō Poppaeae respondit,
'tū nūbem cōnspexistī. sed ego cinerem
sēnsī. ego flammās vīdī.'

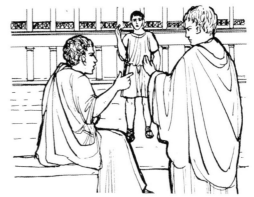

7 Marcus et Quārtus in forō erant. Sulla ad
frātrēs contendit.

8 Sulla frātribus dīxit,
'ego ad theātrum contendēbam. ego
sonōs audīvī et tremōrēs sēnsī. vōs sonōs
audīvistis? vōs tremōrēs sēnsistis?'

9 frātrēs Sullae respondērunt,
'nōs tremōrēs sēnsimus et sonōs
audīvimus. nōs nūbem mīrābilem
vīdimus. nōs sollicitī sumus.'

tremōrēs

tremōrēs *tremors*

When you have read this story, answer the questions opposite.

Caecilius cum Iūliō cēnābat. Iūlius in vīllā splendidā prope
Nūceriam habitābat.

    Iūlius Caeciliō dīxit, 'ego sollicitus sum. ego in hortō heri
ambulābam et librum legēbam. subitō terra valdē tremuit. ego
tremōrēs sēnsī. quid tū agēbās?'   5

    'ego servō epistulās dictābam', inquit Caecilius. 'ego quoque
tremōrēs sēnsī. postquam terra tremuit, Grumiō tablīnum
intrāvit et mē ad hortum dūxit. nōs nūbem mīrābilem vīdimus.'

    'vōs timēbātis?' rogāvit Iūlius.

    'nōs nōn timēbāmus', Caecilius Iūliō respondit. 'ego,   10
postquam nūbem cōnspexī, familiam meam ad larārium vocāvī.
tum nōs laribus sacrificium fēcimus.'

    'hercle! vōs fortissimī erātis', clāmāvit Iūlius. 'vōs tremōrēs
sēnsistis, vōs nūbem cōnspexistis. vōs tamen nōn erātis
perterritī.'   15

    'nōs nōn timēbāmus, quod nōs laribus crēdēbāmus', inquit
Caecilius. 'iamprīdem terra tremuit. iamprīdem tremōrēs vīllās
et mūrōs dēlēvērunt. sed larēs vīllam meam et familiam meam
servāvērunt. ego igitur sollicitus nōn sum.'

    subitō servus triclīnium intrāvit.   20

    'domine, Clēmēns est in ātriō. Clēmēns ex urbe vēnit.
Caecilium quaerit', servus Iūliō dīxit.

    'nōn intellegō', Caecilius exclāmāvit. 'ego Clēmentem ad
fundum meum māne mīsī.'

    servus Clēmentem in triclīnium dūxit.   25

    'cūr tū ē fundō discessistī? cūr tū ad hanc vīllam vēnistī?'
rogāvit Caecilius.

    Clēmēns dominō et Iūliō rem tōtam nārrāvit.

---

tremuit *shook*
sēnsī *felt*
agēbās *were doing*
epistulās *letters*
dictābam *was dictating*
nūbem *cloud*

familiam *household*
larārium *shrine of the household gods*
laribus *household gods*
sacrificium *sacrifice*

iamprīdem *a long time ago*

fundum *farm*

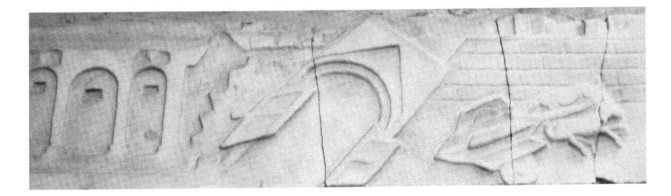

Questions

		Marks
1	What was Caecilius doing at the beginning of this story? Where was he?	2
2	Why was Iulius worried?	1
3	What was Caecilius doing when the tremors began (line 6)?	1
4	What did Caecilius say that he and Grumio had seen when they went into the garden?	1
5	What two things did Caecilius say he had done next (lines 11–12)?	2
6	Why did Iulius think that Caecilius and his household were **fortissimī** (line 13)?	3
7	Why was Caecilius so sure that his Lares (gods) would look after his household (lines 17–19)?	3
8	**subitō servus triclīnium intrāvit** (line 20). What news did he bring?	3
9	What was Caecilius' reaction to the news? Why did he react in this way?	2
10	Read the last three lines of the story. Why do you think Clemens has come?	2

TOTAL **20**

This is how Caecilius would have pictured a Lar, one of the gods who guarded his household.

Below and opposite: *At the time of the eruption, Caecilius' lararium was decorated with marble pictures of the earthquake that happened in AD 62.*

ad urbem

'ego ad fundum tuum contendī', Clēmēns dominō dīxit. 'ego
vīlicō epistulam tuam trādidī. postquam vīlicus epistulam lēgit,
nōs fundum et servōs īnspiciēbāmus. subitō nōs ingentēs sonōs
audīvimus. nōs tremōrēs quoque sēnsimus. tum ego montem
spectāvī et nūbem mīrābilem vīdī.'   5

'quid vōs fēcistis?' rogāvit Iūlius.

'nōs urbem petīvimus, quod valdē timēbāmus', respondit
Clēmēns. 'ego, postquam urbem intrāvī, clāmōrem ingentem
audīvī. multī Pompēiānī per viās currēbant. fēminae cum
īnfantibus per urbem festīnābant. fīliī et fīliae parentēs   10
quaerēbant. ego ad vīllam nostram pervēnī, ubi Metella et
Quīntus manēbant. Quīntus mē ad tē mīsit, quod nōs omnēs
perterritī erāmus.'

Caecilius ad urbem contendit, quod sollicitus erat. Iūlius et
Clēmēns quoque ad urbem festīnāvērunt. maxima turba viās   15
complēbat, quod Pompēiānī ē vīllīs festīnābant.

prope urbem Holcōnium cōnspexērunt. Holcōnius cum
servīs ad portum fugiēbat.

'cūr vōs ad urbem contenditis? cūr nōn ad portum fugitis?'
rogāvit Holcōnius.   20

'ad vīllam meam contendō', Caecilius Holcōniō respondit.
'Metellam et Quīntum quaerō. tū Metellam vīdistī? Quīntum
cōnspexistī?'

'ēheu!' clāmāvit Holcōnius. 'ego vīllam splendidam
habēbam. in vīllā erant statuae pulchrae et pictūrae pretiōsae.   25
iste mōns vīllam meam dēlēvit; omnēs statuae sunt frāctae.'

'sed, amīce, tū uxōrem meam vīdistī?' rogāvit Caecilius.

'ego nihil dē Metellā scio. nihil cūrō', respondit Holcōnius.

'furcifer!' clāmāvit Caecilius. 'tū vīllam tuam āmīsistī. ego
uxōrem meam āmīsī!'   30

Caecilius, postquam Holcōnium vituperāvit, ad urbem
contendit.

vīlicō *farm manager, bailiff*
sonōs *noises*

fīliae *daughters*
parentēs *parents*
pervēnī *reached, arrived at*

pretiōsae *precious*
iste mōns *that (terrible)*
              mountain
scio *know*
nihil cūrō *I don't care*

ad vīllam

in urbe pavor maximus erat. cinis iam dēnsior incidēbat. flammae ubīque erant. Caecilius et amīcī, postquam urbem intrāvērunt, vīllam petēbant. sed iter erat difficile, quod multī Pompēiānī viās complēbant. Caecilius tamen per viās fortiter contendēbat.

nūbēs iam dēnsissima erat. subitō Iūlius exclāmāvit,
'vōs ad vīllam contendite! ego nōn valeō.'

statim ad terram dēcidit exanimātus. Clēmēns Iūlium ad templum proximum portāvit.

'tū optimē fēcistī', Caecilius servō dīxit. 'tū Iūlium servāvistī. ego tibi lībertātem prōmittō.'

tum Caecilius ē templō discessit et ad vīllam cucurrit.

Clēmēns cum Iūliō in templō manēbat. tandem Iūlius respīrāvit.

'ubi sumus?' rogāvit.

'sumus tūtī', servus Iūliō respondit. 'dea Īsis nōs servāvit. postquam tū in terram dēcidistī, ego tē ad hoc templum portāvī.'

'tibi grātiās maximās agō, quod tū mē servāvistī', inquit Iūlius. 'sed ubi est Caecilius?'

'dominus meus ad vīllam contendit', respondit Clēmēns.

'ēheu! stultissimus est Caecilius!' clāmāvit Iūlius. 'sine dubiō Metella et Quīntus mortuī sunt. ego ex urbe quam celerrimē discēdō. tū mēcum venīs?'

'minimē, amīce!' Clēmēns Iūliō respondit. 'ego dominum meum quaerō!'

---

pavor *panic*
cinis *ash*
iam *now*
dēnsior *thicker*
5   incidēbat *was falling*
flammae *flames*
iter *journey, progress*
difficile *difficult*
valeō *I feel well*
10   dēcidit *fell down*
exanimātus *unconscious*
templum *temple*
proximum *nearest*
lībertātem *freedom*
15   respīrāvit *recovered breath,*
     recovered consciousness
tūtī *safe*
dea *goddess*

20

sine dubiō *without doubt*

25

The goddess Isis, on a ring.

The temple of Isis, Pompeii.

fīnis

iam nūbēs ātra ad terram dēscendēbat; iam cinis dēnsissimus incidēbat. plūrimī Pompēiānī iam dē urbe suā dēspērābant. Clēmēns tamen nōn dēspērābat, sed obstinātē vīllam petīvit, quod Caecilium quaerēbat. tandem ad vīllam pervēnit. sollicitus ruīnās spectāvit. tōta vīlla ardēbat. Clēmēns fūmum ubīque vīdit. per ruīnās tamen fortiter contendit et dominum suum vocāvit. Caecilius tamen nōn respondit. subitō canis lātrāvit. servus tablīnum intrāvit, ubi canis erat. Cerberus dominum custōdiēbat.

Caecilius in tablīnō moribundus iacēbat. mūrus sēmirutus eum paene cēlābat. Clēmēns dominō vīnum dedit. Caecilius, postquam vīnum bibit, sēnsim respīrāvit.

'quid accidit, domine?' rogāvit Clēmēns.

'ego ad vīllam vēnī', inquit Caecilius. 'Metellam nōn vīdī! Quīntum nōn vīdī! vīlla erat dēserta. tum ego ad tablīnum contendēbam. subitō terra tremuit et pariēs in mē incidit. tū es servus fidēlis. abī! ego tē iubeō. dē vītā meā dēspērō. Metella et Quīntus periērunt. nunc ego quoque sum moritūrus.'

Clēmēns recūsāvit. in tablīnō obstinātē manēbat. Caecilius iterum clāmāvit,

'Clēmēns, abī! tē iubeō. fortasse Quīntus superfuit. quaere Quīntum! hunc ānulum Quīntō dā!'

Caecilius, postquam Clēmentī ānulum suum trādidit, statim exspīrāvit. Clēmēns dominō trīste 'valē' dīxit et ē vīllā discessit.

Cerberus tamen in vīllā mānsit. dominum frūstrā custōdiēbat.

---

fīnis *end*

ātra *black*
dēscendēbat *was coming down*
plūrimī *most*
obstinātē *stubbornly*
5   ruīnās *ruins, wreckage*
fūmum *smoke*

10   moribundus *almost dead*
sēmirutus *half-collapsed*
sēnsim *slowly, gradually*
accidit *happened*

15

pariēs *wall*
iubeō *order*
periērunt *have died, have perished*
20   moritūrus *going to die*
recūsāvit *refused*
superfuit *has survived*

exspīrāvit *died*
25   trīste *sadly*

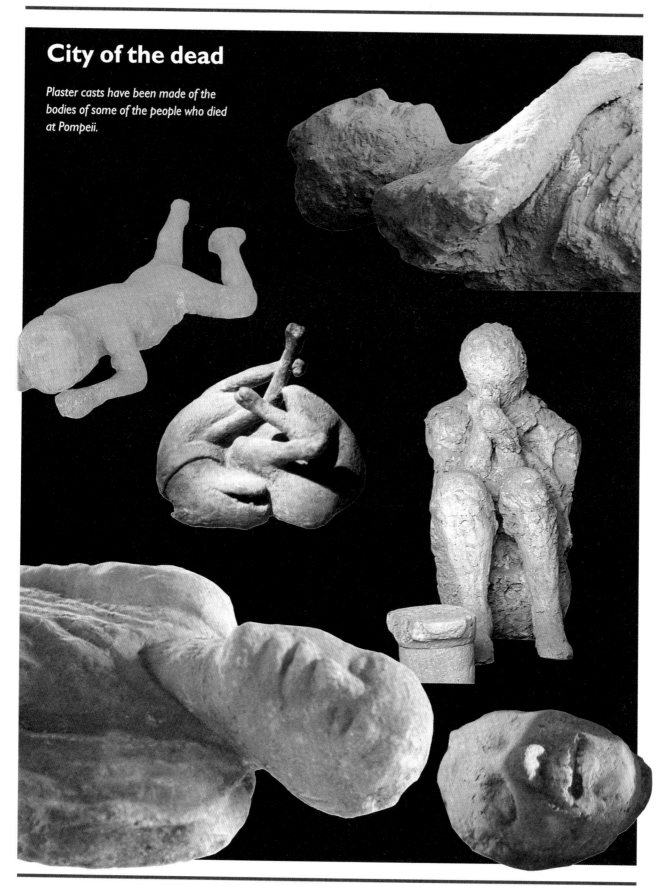

City of the dead

Plaster casts have been made of the bodies of some of the people who died at Pompeii.

About the language

1 In Stage 6 you met the imperfect and perfect tenses:

IMPERFECT		PERFECT	
portābat	*s/he was carrying*	portāvit	*s/he carried*
portābant	*they were carrying*	portāvērunt	*they carried*

2 In Stage 12, you have met the imperfect and perfect tenses with *I, you* and *we*:

IMPERFECT		PERFECT	
(ego) portābam	*I was carrying*	(ego) portāvī	*I carried*
(tū) portābās	*you (singular) were carrying*	(tū) portāvistī	*you (singular) carried*
(nōs) portābāmus	*we were carrying*	(nōs) portāvimus	*we carried*
(vōs) portābātis	*you (plural) were carrying*	(vōs) portāvistis	*you (plural) carried*

ego, tū, nōs and **vōs** are used only for emphasis and are usually left out.

3 The full imperfect and perfect tenses are:

IMPERFECT		PERFECT	
(ego)	portābam	(ego)	portāvī
(tū)	portābās	(tū)	portāvistī
	portābat		portāvit
(nōs)	portābāmus	(nōs)	portāvimus
(vōs)	portābātis	(vōs)	portāvistis
	portābant		portāvērunt

4 The words for *was* and *were* are as follows:

(ego)	eram	*I was*
(tū)	erās	*you (singular) were*
	erat	*s/he was*
(nōs)	erāmus	*we were*
(vōs)	erātis	*you (plural) were*
	erant	*they were*

5 Further examples:

a portāvistis; portābātis; portābāmus
b trāxī; trāxērunt; trāxistī
c docēbant; docuī; docuimus
d erātis; audīvī; trahēbam

The terrible mountain

Right: *A Pompeian painting of Vesuvius as Caecilius knew it, with vineyards on its fertile slopes.*

Below: *The mountain erupting in the eighteenth century; steam rising in the crater today; and the view from the sea, with the central cone replaced by two lower summits.*

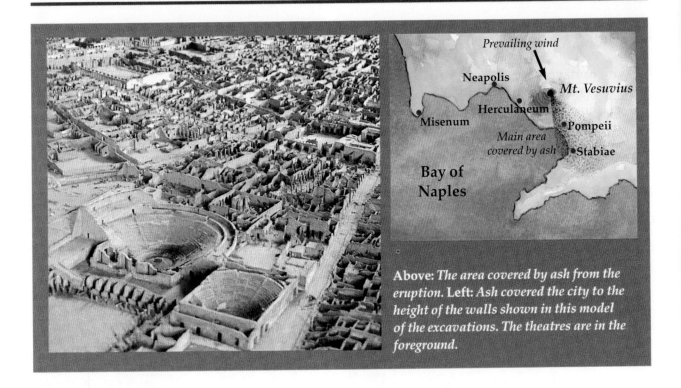

Above: *The area covered by ash from the eruption.* Left: *Ash covered the city to the height of the walls shown in this model of the excavations. The theatres are in the foreground.*

The destruction and excavation of Pompeii

On the night of 23–4 August, AD 79, it rained hard; a strong wind blew and earth tremors were felt. During the following morning, Vesuvius, which had been an inactive volcano for many centuries, erupted with enormous violence, devastating much of the surrounding area. A huge mass of mud poured down the mountainside and swallowed the town of Herculaneum; hot stones and ash descended in vast quantities on Pompeii, burying everything to a depth of four-and-a-half to six metres (15–20 feet). Most people, with vivid memories of the earthquake of seventeen years before, fled into the open countryside carrying a few possessions, but others remained behind, hoping that the storm would pass. They died, buried in the ruins of their homes or suffocated by sulphur fumes.

The next day, the whole of Pompeii was a desert of white ash. Here and there the tops of buildings could be seen, and little groups of survivors struggled back to salvage what they could. They dug tunnels to get down to their homes and rescue money, furniture and other valuables. But nothing could be done to excavate and rebuild the town itself. The site was abandoned; thousands of refugees made new homes in Naples and other

Campanian towns. Gradually the ruins collapsed, a new layer of soil covered the site and Pompeii disappeared from view.

During the Middle Ages, nobody knew exactly where the town lay. Only a vague memory survived in the name 'civitá' by which the local people still called the low hill. But what city it was or whether there really was a city buried there, they neither knew nor cared.

The rediscovery of Pompeii and Herculaneum

The first remains of Pompeii were found in 1594, when an Italian architect called Fontana was constructing a water channel from the River Sarno to a nearby town. He discovered the remains of buildings and an inscription. But these were misunderstood as it was thought that a villa belonging to the famous Roman politician, Pompeius, had been discovered. Nothing much was done for another 150 years, until in 1748, Charles III, King of Naples, began to excavate the site in search of treasure. In 1763, the treasure seekers realised they were exploring the lost city of Pompeii. At Herculaneum the excavations were much more difficult because the volcanic mud had turned to hard rock and the town lay up to twelve metres (forty feet) below the new ground level. Tunnelling down was slow and dangerous work.

In the early days of excavation, no effort was made to uncover the sites in an orderly way; the methods of modern archaeology were unknown. The excavators were not interested in uncovering towns in order to learn about the people who had lived there, but were looking for jewellery, statues and other works of art, which were then taken away to decorate the palaces of kings and rich men.

Herculaneum. In the foreground are some of the excavated Roman buildings. The modern buildings in the distance lie above the unexcavated part of the town. The first floor of houses survives here.

A table is still in place in an upper room.

Uncovering the temple of Isis in 1765.

At the beginning of the nineteenth century, however, the looting was stopped and systematic excavation began. Section by section, the soil and rubble were cleared. The most fragile and precious objects were taken to the National Museum in Naples, but everything else was kept where it was found. As buildings were uncovered, they were partly reconstructed with original materials to preserve them and make them safe for visitors.

From time to time, archaeologists found a hollow space in the solidified ash where an object of wood or other organic material perished. To find out what it was they poured liquid plaster into the hole, and when it hardened they carefully removed the surrounding ash, and were left with a perfect image of the original object. This work still continues, but now resin is used instead of plaster. In this way, many wooden doors and shutters have been discovered, and also bodies of human beings and animals.

A resin cast of a young woman's body. Unlike plaster, resin is transparent and bones and jewellery can be seen through it. Resin is also less fragile than plaster.

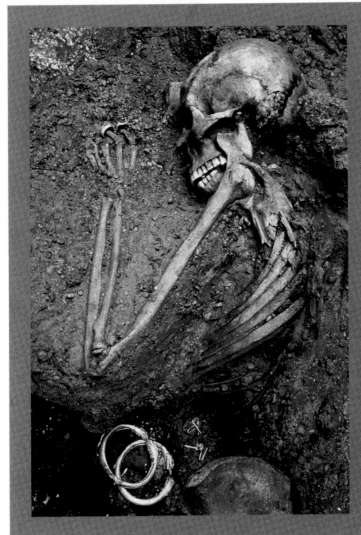

Nowadays every bone and object discovered is carefully examined, recorded and conserved. This skeleton was discovered at Herculaneum in 1982. The bones showed that she was a woman of about 45, with a protruding jaw; she had gum disease but no cavities in her teeth. Her wealth was clear from her rings and the bracelets and earrings (below) that had been in her purse. By contrast, the bones of slaves may show signs of overwork and undernourishment.

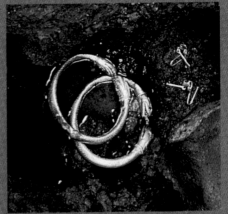

The people died – the garden lives

Below: *Plaster casts are also made of tree-roots, which helps identify the trees planted in the gardens and orchards of Pompeii. The position of each vine in this vineyard was identified and it has now been replanted.*
Right: *In the corner of the vineyard, just inside the walls, huddles a group of adults and children that failed to get away.*

At Herculaneum, where the town was hermetically sealed by the solidified mud, perishable objects have survived intact, for example, wooden doors and stairs, woven material, fishermen's nets and wax tablets.

The work is not yet finished. Only about three-fifths of Pompeii have so far been uncovered and less of Herculaneum. Whenever a new house is opened up, the archaeologists find it just as it was abandoned. They may discover the remains of a meal, pots on the stove, coins in the tablinum, lampstands in various rooms, wall-paintings (often only slightly damaged), the lead pipes which supplied water to the fountains in the garden, brooches, needles, jars of cosmetics, shoes and toys; in fact all the hundreds of small things that went to make up a Roman home. If they are lucky, they may also discover the name of the family that lived there.

Thus, through the efforts of archaeologists, a remarkably detailed picture of the life of this ordinary Roman town has emerged from the disaster which destroyed it 2,000 years ago.

Vocabulary checklist 12

āmittit	*loses*
complet	*fills*
custōdit	*guards*
epistula	*letter*
flamma	*flame*
fortiter	*bravely*
frūstrā	*in vain*
fugit	*runs away, flees*
fundus	*farm*
iacet	*lies*
iam	*now*
igitur	*therefore*
mīrābilis	*strange, extraordinary*
mittit	*sends*
mōns	*mountain*
optimē	*very well*
paene	*nearly, almost*
sentit	*feels*
tandem	*at last*
templum	*temple*
terra	*ground, land*
timet	*is afraid, fears*

You have also met these numbers:

ūnus	*one*
duo	*two*
trēs	*three*

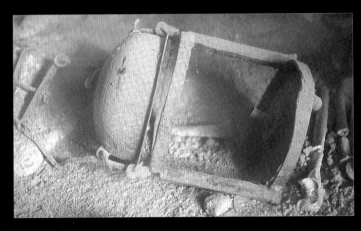

An abandoned lantern, with the bones of its owner.

LANGUAGE INFORMATION

Contents

Part One: About the Language

Nouns

1   In Book I, you have met the following cases:

	first declension	*second declension*	*third declension*	
SINGULAR				
nominative	puella	servus	mercātor	leō
accusative	puellam	servum	mercātōrem	leōnem
dative	puellae	servō	mercātōrī	leōnī
PLURAL				
nominative	puellae	servī	mercātōrēs	leōnēs
accusative	puellās	servōs	mercātōrēs	leōnēs
dative	puellīs	servīs	mercātōribus	leōnibus

2   Notice again the way the cases are used:

nominative   **mercātor** cantābat.
The merchant was singing.

servī labōrābant.
The slaves were working.

accusative   Grumiō **puellam** salūtāvit.
Grumio greeted the girl.

Caecilius **servōs** vituperāvit.
Caecilius cursed the slaves.

dative   senex **mercātōrī** pictūram ostendit.
The old man showed the painting to the merchant.

lībertī **puellīs** vīnum trādidērunt.
The freedmen handed over the wine to the girls.

3 Change the word in **bold** type from the singular to the plural, and translate the new sentence.

> For example: puerī **servum** vīdērunt.
> This becomes: puerī **servōs** vīdērunt.
> Translation: *The boys saw the slaves.*

   a puerī **leōnem** vīdērunt.
   b dominus **puellam** audīvit.
   c centuriō **amīcum** salūtāvit.
   d cīvēs **servō** pecūniam trādidērunt.
   e coquus **mercātōrī** cēnam parāvit.

4 Change the word in **bold** type from the plural to the singular, and translate the new sentence.

> For example: vēnālīciī **mercātōribus** pecūniam dedērunt.
> This becomes: vēnālīciī **mercātōrī** pecūniam dedērunt.
> Translation: *The slave-dealers gave money to the merchant.*

   a dominus **servōs** īnspexit.
   b āthlētae **mercātōrēs** vituperāvērunt.
   c vēnālīcius **ancillās** vēndēbat.
   d gladiātōrēs **leōnibus** cibum dedērunt.
   e iuvenēs **puellīs** statuam ostendērunt.

Verbs

1 In Book I, you have met the following forms of the verb:

PRESENT TENSE		
	portō	*I carry*
	portās	*you (sing.) carry*
	portat	*s/he carries*
	portāmus	*we carry*
	portātis	*you (plural) carry*
	portant	*they carry*

IMPERFECT TENSE		
	portābam	*I was carrying*
	portābās	*you (sing.) were carrying*
	portābat	*s/he was carrying*
	portābāmus	*we were carrying*
	portābātis	*you (plural) were carrying*
	portābant	*they were carrying*

PERFECT TENSE		
	portāvī	*I carried*
	portāvistī	*you (sing.) carried*
	portāvit	*s/he carried*
	portāvimus	*we carried*
	portāvistis	*you (plural) carried*
	portāvērunt	*they carried*

2 English has more than one way of translating each of these tenses.

- The present tense **portō** can mean either *I carry* or *I am carrying*.

- The imperfect tense **portābam** can mean either *I was carrying* or I *used to carry* or sometimes I *began to carry*.

- The perfect tense **portāvī** can mean *I carried* or *I have carried*.

3 Latin verbs belong to groups known as conjugations.

- **portō** *I carry* is an example of a first conjugation verb. Further examples: **ambulō** and **labōrō**.

- **doceō** *I teach* is an example of a second conjugation verb. Further examples: **sedeō** and **videō**.

- **trahō** *I drag* is an example of a third conjugation verb.
  Further examples: **currō** and **dīcō.**

- **audiō** *I hear* is an example of a fourth conjugation verb.
  Further examples: **dormiō** and **veniō.**

4   The full table of verb endings met in Book I is as follows:

	first conjugation	*second conjugation*	*third conjugation*	*fourth conjugation*
PRESENT TENSE	portō	doceō	trahō	audiō
	portās	docēs	trahis	audīs
	portat	docet	trahit	audit
	portāmus	docēmus	trahimus	audīmus
	portātis	docētis	trahitis	audītis
	portant	docent	trahunt	audiunt
IMPERFECT TENSE	portābam	docēbam	trahēbam	audiēbam
	portābās	docēbās	trahēbās	audiēbās
	portābat	docēbat	trahēbat	audiēbat
	portābāmus	docēbāmus	trahēbāmus	audiēbāmus
	portābātis	docēbātis	trahēbātis	audiēbātis
	portābant	docēbant	trahēbant	audiēbant
PERFECT TENSE	portāvī	docuī	trāxī	audīvī
	portāvistī	docuistī	trāxistī	audīvistī
	portāvit	docuit	trāxit	audīvit
	portāvimus	docuimus	trāximus	audīvimus
	portāvistis	docuistis	trāxistis	audīvistis
	portāvērunt	docuērunt	trāxērunt	audīvērunt

5   In paragraph 4 above, find the Latin words for:

a I teach; we drag; he hears.
b She was dragging; you (plural) were teaching; they were carrying.
c He heard; they dragged; we taught.
d We heard; you (sing.) teach; they were dragging; she carried.

6 Translate these examples:

    a ego sedeō; ancilla sedet; nōs sedēmus; amīcī sedent.

    b servī labōrābant; tū labōrābās; servus labōrābat; ego labōrābam.

    c canēs dormīvērunt; tū dormīvistī; dormīvit; nōs dormīvimus.

    d servus clāmat; servus clāmābat; servus clāmāvit.

    e clāmās; clāmābat; clāmāvistis.

    f dīxērunt; dīcis; dīcēbamus.

    g parat; appārēbātis; intrābam.

    h vidēmus; currēbās; veniēbant; labōrāvī.

7 A few verbs which do not belong to any of the four conjugations are known as irregular verbs. This is the most important one:

PRESENT TENSE		IMPERFECT TENSE	
sum	*I am*	eram	*I was*
es	*you (sing.) are*	erās	*you (sing.) were*
est	*s/he is*	erat	*s/he was*
sumus	*we are*	erāmus	*we were*
estis	*you (plural) are*	erātis	*you (plural) were*
sunt	*they are*	erant	*they were*

Ways of forming the perfect tense

1 Most verbs in the first, second and fourth conjugations form their perfect tenses in the following ways:

   First conjugation: like **portāvī**, e.g. **salūtāvī**
   Second conjugation: like **docuī**, e.g. **terruī, appāruī**
   Fourth conjugation: like **audīvī**, e.g. **dormīvī, custōdīvī.**

2 Some verbs in the third conjugation form their perfect tense in the same way as **trāxī**, e.g. **dīxī, intellēxī.** But there are many other ways in which verbs, especially in the third conjugation, may form their perfect tense. Note the following examples:

PRESENT		PERFECT	
discēdo	*I leave*	discessī	*I left*
mittō	*I send*	mīsī	*I sent*
currō	*I run*	cucurrī	*I ran*
faciō	*I make*	fēcī	*I made*
capiō	*I take*	cēpī	*I took*
videō	*I see*	vīdī	*I saw*
veniō	*I come*	vēnī	*I came*

Word order

1   The following word order is very common in Latin:

       Milō discum īnspexit.   *Milo looked at the discus.*
       mercātor togam vēndidit.   *The merchant sold the toga.*

2   From Stage 7 onwards, you have met a slightly different example:

       discum īnspexit.   *He looked at the discus.*
       togam vēndidit.   *He sold the toga.*
       amīcum salūtāvit.   *He greeted his friend.*
       theātrum intrāvērunt.   *They entered the theatre.*

3   The following sentences are similar to those in paragraphs 1 and 2:

    a   spectātōrēs Milōnem laudāvērunt.
    b   Milōnem laudāvērunt.
    c   senex agricolam cōnspexit.
    d   agricolam cōnspexit.
    e   canēs et servī leōnem necāvērunt.
    f   mercātor poētam et vēnālīcium vīdit.
    g   poētam vīdit.
    h   āthlētam salūtāvit.
    i   mē salūtāvit.
    j   tē salūtāvērunt.
    k   Metella clāmōrem audīvit.
    l   clāmōrem audīvit.

4   Further examples:

    a   Caecilius amīcum salūtat; amīcum salūtat.
    b   ego amīcōs salūtāvī; amīcōs salūtāvī.
    c   nōs gladiātōrēs spectābāmus; clāmōrem audīvimus.
    d   vōs cibum cōnsūmēbātis; vīnum bibēbātis; Grumiōnem laudāvistis.

5   From Stage 9 onwards, you have met longer sentences, involving the dative. The following word order is common in Latin:

vēnālīcius mercātōrī ancillam ostendit.
The slave-dealer showed the slave-girl to the merchant.

6   Further examples:

a   iuvenis Milōnī discum trādidit.
b   Metella fīliō dōnum ēmit.
c   dominus ancillīs signum dedit.
d   nūntiī cīvibus spectāculum nūntiāvērunt.
e   Quīntus mercātōrī et amīcīs togam ostendit.

Longer sentences with postquam and quod

1 Compare these two sentences:

Pompēiānī gladiātōrēs vīdērunt.
The Pompeians saw the gladiators.

Pompēiānī, postquam amphitheātrum intrāvērunt, gladiātōrēs vīdērunt.
The Pompeians, after they entered the amphitheatre, saw the gladiators.

Or, in more natural English:
After the Pompeians entered the amphitheatre, they saw the gladiators.

2 The next example is similar:

servī umbram timēbant.
The slaves were afraid of the ghost.

servī, quod erant ignāvī, umbram timēbant.
The slaves, because they were cowardly, were afraid of the ghost.

Or:
Because the slaves were cowardly, they were afraid of the ghost.

3 Further examples:

a Metella ad tablīnum festīnāvit.
  Metella, postquam ē culīnā discessit, ad tablīnum festīnāvit.
b amīcī Fēlīcem laudāvērunt.
  amīcī, postquam fābulam audīvērunt, Fēlīcem laudāvērunt.
c tuba sonuit.
  postquam Rēgulus signum dedit, tuba sonuit.
d Caecilius nōn erat sollicitus.
  Caecilius nōn erat sollicitus, quod in cubiculō dormiēbat.
e Nūcerīnī fūgērunt.
  Nūcerīnī, quod Pompēiānī erant īrātī, fūgērunt.

Part Two: Vocabulary

1   Nouns are usually listed in the form of their nominative singular.
    For example:

    servus   *slave*

2   Third declension nouns are usually listed with both nominative and accusative
    singular. For example:

    leō: leōnem   *lion*

    This means that **leō** is the nominative singular and **leōnem** the accusative
    singular of the word for 'lion'.

3   *Practice examples*

    Find the nominative singular of the following words:

    novāculam
    lupum
    sanguinem
    stēllae
    īnfantēs
    mūrō
    cīvibus

4   Verbs are usually listed in the form of their present and perfect tenses.
    For example:

    parat   *prepares:* parāvit

    This means that **parat** means 's/he prepares' and **parāvit** means 's/he prepared'.

5   If only one of these two tenses is used in Book I, then only that tense is listed.
    For example:

    exspīrāvit   *died*

6 *Practice examples*

Find the meaning of the following words, some of which are in the present tense and some in the perfect:

> laudat
> laudāvit
> salūtāvit
> intellēxit
> tenet
> accēpit

7 Some Latin words have more than one possible translation. Always choose the most suitable translation for the sentence you are working on.

> cīvēs perterritī urbem petēbant.
> *The terrified citizens were making for the city.*

> iuvenēs īrātī mercātōrem petīvērunt.
> *The angry young men attacked the merchant.*

8 All words which are given in the checklists for Stages 1–12 are marked with an asterisk (*) in the following pages.

a

* abest — is out, is absent
* abit — goes away: abiit
  accidit — happened
* accipit — accepts: accēpit
  accūsat — accuses
  āctor: āctōrem — actor
* ad — to, at
  addidit — added
* adest — is here
  adiuvat — helps
  administrat — looks after
  aedificat — builds
  aeger: aegrum — sick, ill
  Aegyptius — Egyptian
* agit — does, acts
    fābulam agit — acts a play
    grātiās agit — thanks, gives thanks
    negōtium agit — does business, works
* agitat — chases, hunts: agitāvit
* agnōscit — recognises: agnōvit
* agricola — farmer
  alius — other, another
  alter: alterum — the other, the second
* ambulat — walks: ambulāvit
  amīcissimus — very friendly
* amīcus — friend
* āmittit — loses: āmīsit
  amphitheātrum — amphitheatre
* ancilla — slave-girl, maid
  antīquus — old, ancient
* ānulus — ring
  anxius — anxious
  aperit — opens: aperuit
  apodytērium — changing-room
  appāret — appears: appāruit
  architectus — builder, architect
  ardet — burns, is on fire
  arēna — arena
  argentāria — banker's stall
  argentārius — banker
  argūmentum — proof, evidence
  artifex: artificem — artist, craftsman
  asinus — ass, donkey
  āter: ātrum — black
  āthlēta — athlete
  ātrium — atrium, main room
  attonitus — astonished
  auctor: auctōrem — creator
  audācissimē — very boldly
* audit — hears, listens to: audīvit
  aurae — air
  auxilium — help
  avārus — miser

b

  babae! — hey!
  barba — beard
  barbarus — barbarian
  basilica — law court
  benignus — kind
  bēstia — wild beast
  bēstiārius — a gladiator who fights animals, beast-fighter
* bibit — drinks: bibit

c

  caelum — sky
* callidus — clever, cunning
    callidior — more cunning, cleverer
  candidātus — candidate
* canis: canem — dog
  cantat — sings: cantāvit
* capit — takes: cēpit
  caudex: caudicem — blockhead, idiot
  caupō: caupōnem — innkeeper
  cautē — cautiously
  cēlat — hides: cēlāvit
  celebrat — celebrates
* celeriter — quickly
    quam celerrimē — as quickly as possible
* cēna — dinner
* cēnat — dines, has dinner: cēnāvit
  centuriō: centuriōnem — centurion
  cēpit — took
  cēra — wax, wax tablet
  cervus — deer
  Chrīstiānus — Christian

* cibus	food		
cinis: cinerem	ash		
* circumspectat	looks round: circumspectāvit	—————— **d** ——————	
* cīvis: cīvem	citizen		
* clāmat	shouts: clāmāvit	* dat	gives: dedit
* clāmor: clāmōrem	shout, uproar	fābulam dat	puts on a play
clausit	shut, closed	* dē	down from; about
clausus	closed	dea	goddess
cōgitat	considers	dēbet	owes
columba	dove	decem	ten
commīsit	began	dēcidit	fell down
commōtus	moved, affected	dēcipit	deceives, fools
* complet	fills	dedit	gave, has given
compōnit	arranges	dēiēcit	threw down
comprehendit	arrested	deinde	then
cōnfēcit	finished	dēlectat	delights, pleases: dēlectāvit
cōnsentit	agrees	dēlēvit	destroyed
cōnsilium	plan, idea	dēliciae	darling
cōnsilium capit	makes a plan, has an idea	dēnārius	a denarius (coin)
* cōnspicit	catches sight of: cōnspexit	dēnsus	thick
* cōnsūmit	eats: cōnsūmpsit	dēnsior	thicker
* contendit	hurries: contendit	dēnsissimus	very thick
contentiō: contentiōnem	argument	dēpōnit	puts down, takes off: dēposuit
* contentus	satisfied	dēscendit	comes down
contrōversia	debate	dēsertus	deserted
* convenit	gathers, meets	dēsistit	stops
convincit	convicts, finds guilty	dēspērat	despairs
* coquit	cooks: coxit	dēstrīnxit	drew out
* coquus	cook	deus	god
cotīdiē	every day	dīcit	says: dīxit
* crēdit	trusts, believes, has faith in	dictat	dictates
		* diēs: diem	day
crīnēs: crīnēs	hair	diēs nātālis: diem nātālem	birthday
* cubiculum	bedroom	difficilis	difficult
cucurrit	ran	dīligenter	carefully
culīna	kitchen	discēdit	departs, leaves: discessit
* cum	with	discit	learns
* cupit	wants	discus	discus
* cūr?	why?	dissentit	disagrees, argues
cūrat	looks after	dīves: dīvitem	rich
nihil cūrō	I don't care	dīvīsor: dīvīsōrem	distributor, a man hired to bribe electors
* currit	runs: cucurrit	dīxit	said
* custōdit	guards: custōdīvit	docet	teaches
		doctus	educated, skilful
		dolet	hurts, is in pain

domina	*mistress, madam*
* dominus	*master*
dōnum	*present, gift*
* dormit	*sleeps:* dormīvit
dubium	*doubt*
* dūcit	*leads, takes:* dūxit
* duo	*two*

e

* ē	*from, out of*
eam	*her*
ēbrius	*drunk*
* ecce!	*look!*
ēdit	*presents:* ēdidit
effūgit	*escaped*
* ego	*I*
* ēheu!	*oh dear! oh no!*
ēlēgit	*chose*
* emit	*buys:* ēmit
* ēmittit	*throws, sends out:* ēmīsit
eōs	*them*
* epistula	*letter*
ērādit	*rubs out, erases:* ērāsit
erat	*was*
* est	*is*
ēsurit	*is hungry*
* et	*and*
euge!	*hurray!*
* eum	*him, it*
ēvānuit	*vanished*
ēvītāvit	*avoided*
ēvolāvit	*flew*
ex	*out of, from*
exanimātus	*unconscious*
excitāvit	*aroused, woke up*
* exclāmat	*exclaims, shouts:* exclāmāvit
* exit	*goes out*
expedītus	*lightly armed*
explicāvit	*explained*
* exspectat	*waits for*
exspīrāvit	*died*
extrāxit	*pulled out*

f

* fābula	*play, story*
* facile	*easily*
* facit	*makes, does:* fēcit
familia	*household*
fautor: fautōrem	*supporter*
* favet	*favours, supports*
fēcit	*made, did*
fēlēs: fēlem	*cat*
fēlīx: fēlīcem	*lucky*
* fēmina	*woman*
* ferōciter	*fiercely*
* ferōx: ferōcem	*fierce, ferocious*
ferōcissimus	*very fierce*
* fert	*brings, carries*
* festīnat	*hurries:* festīnāvit
fidēlis	*faithful, loyal*
fīlia	*daughter*
* fīlius	*son*
fīnis: fīnem	*end*
* flamma	*flame*
fluit	*flows*
fortasse	*perhaps*
* fortis	*brave*
fortior	*braver*
fortissimus	*very brave*
* fortiter	*bravely*
forum	*forum, market-place*
frāctus	*broken*
* frāter: frātrem	*brother*
fremit	*roars:* fremuit
* frūstrā	*in vain*
* fugit	*runs away, flees:* fūgit
fūmus	*smoke*
fūnambulus	*tight-rope walker*
* fundus	*farm*
* fūr: fūrem	*thief*
furcifer!	*scoundrel!*
fūstis: fūstem	*club*

g

gēns: gentem	*family*
gerit	*wears*
gladiātor: gladiātōrem	*gladiator*
*gladius	*sword*
Graecia	*Greece*
Graeculus	*poor Greek*
Graecus	*Greek*
grātiae	*thanks*
grātiās agit	*thanks, gives thanks*
graviter	*seriously*
gustat	*tastes:* gustāvit

h

*habet	*has*
*habitat	*lives*
hae	*these*
haec	*this*
hanc	*this*
hausit	*drained, drank up*
hercle!	*by Hercules! good heavens!*
*heri	*yesterday*
*hic	*this*
hoc	*this*
*hodiē	*today*
*homō: hominem	*human being, man*
*hortus	*garden*
*hospes: hospitem	*guest*
hūc	*here, to here*
hunc	*this*

i

*iacet	*lies*
*iam	*now*
iamprīdem	*a long time ago*
*iānua	*door*
ībat	*was going*
ibi	*there*
*igitur	*therefore, and so*

*ignāvus	*cowardly, lazy*
illam	*that*
*ille	*that*
imitātor: imitātōrem	*imitator*
*imperium	*empire*
imprimit	*presses*
*in	*in, on; into, onto*
incendium	*fire, blaze*
incidit	*falls:* incidit
incitat	*urges on, encourages*
induit	*puts on*
īnfāns: īnfantem	*child, baby*
īnfēlīx: īnfēlīcem	*unlucky*
*ingēns: ingentem	*huge*
inimīcus	*enemy*
*inquit	*says, said*
īnsānus	*mad, crazy*
īnscrīptiō: īnscrīptiōnem	*inscription, notice, writing*
*īnspicit	*looks at, inspects, examines:* īnspexit
īnstitor: īnstitōrem	*pedlar, street vendor*
*intellegit	*understands:* intellēxit
*intentē	*closely, carefully*
interfēcit	*killed*
*intrat	*enters:* intrāvit
intrō īte!	*go inside!*
intus	*inside*
*invenit	*finds:* invēnit
*invītat	*invites:* invītāvit
*īrātus	*angry*
īrātior	*angrier*
īrātissimus	*very angry*
iste	*that*
*it	*goes:* iit
ita	*in this way*
ita vērō	*yes*
iter	*journey, progress*
*iterum	*again*
iubet	*orders*
*iūdex: iūdicem	*judge*
*iuvenis: iuvenem	*young man*

l

*labōrat	works: labōrāvit
*lacrimat	weeps, cries
laetē	happily
*laetus	happy
laetissimus	very happy
lambit	licks
lapideus	made of stone
larārium	shrine of the household gods
larēs	household gods
Latīnus	Latin
lātrat	barks: lātrāvit
*laudat	praises: laudāvit
lectus	couch
*legit	reads: lēgit
*leō: leōnem	lion
*liber	book
*līberālis	generous
līberālissimus	very generous
līberāvit	freed, set free
līberī	children
lībertās: lībertātem	freedom
*lībertus	freedman, ex-slave
lingua	tongue, language
locus	place
longē	a long way, far
longus	long
longissimus	very long
lūcet	shines
lūna	moon
lupus	wolf

m

magnificē	magnificently
magnificus	magnificent
*magnus	big, large, great
maior	bigger, larger, greater
māne	in the morning
*manet	remains, stays: mānsit
marītus	husband
*māter: mātrem	mother
maximus	very big, very large, very great

mē	me
mēcum	with me
*medius	middle
melior	better
mendācissimus	very deceitful
*mendāx: mendācem	liar
mēnsa	table
*mercātor: mercātōrem	merchant
*meus	my, mine
mihi	to me
*minimē!	no!
*mīrābilis	extraordinary, strange
miserandus	pitiful, pathetic
missiō: missiōnem	release
*mittit	sends: mīsit
*mōns: montem	mountain
moribundus	almost dead, dying
moritūrus	going to die
mors: mortem	death
*mortuus	dead
*mox	soon
*multus	much, many
murmillō: murmillōnem	heavily armed gladiator
*mūrus	wall

n

*nārrat	tells, relates: nārrāvit
nāsus	nose
nauta	sailor
*nāvis: nāvem	ship
*necat	kills: necāvit
negōtium	business
nēmō: nēminem	no one, nobody
*nihil	nothing
nihil cūrō	I don't care
nimium	too much
nisi	except
nōbilis	noble, of noble birth
nōbīs	to us
*nōn	not
*nōs	we, us
*noster: nostrum	our
nōtus	well known, famous
nōtissimus	very well known
novācula	razor

novus	*new*
nox: noctem	*night*
nūbēs: nūbem	*cloud*
Nūcerīnī	*people of Nuceria*
nūllus	*no*
num?	*surely ... not?*
numerat	*counts*
numquam	*never*
*nunc	*now*
*nūntiat	*announces:* nūntiāvit
*nūntius	*messenger*

───────── **o** ─────────

obdormīvit	*went to sleep*
obstinātē	*stubbornly*
occupātus	*busy*
*offert	*offers*
olfēcit	*smelled, sniffed*
*ōlim	*once, some time ago*
*omnis	*all*
*optimē	*very well*
*optimus	*very good, excellent, best*
ōrātiō: ōrātiōnem	*speech*
*ostendit	*shows:* ostendit
ōtiōsus	*idle, on holiday, on vacation*

───────── **p** ─────────

*paene	*nearly, almost*
palaestra	*palaestra, exercise area*
pānis: pānem	*bread*
*parat	*prepares:* parāvit
parātus	*ready*
parce!	*spare me! have pity on me!*
parēns: parentem	*parent*
pariēs: parietem	*wall*
*parvus	*small, little*
pāstor: pāstōrem	*shepherd*
*pater: patrem	*father*
pauper: pauperem	*poor*
pauperrimus	*very poor*
pāvō: pāvōnem	*peacock*
pavor: pavōrem	*panic*

*pāx: pācem	*peace*
*pecūnia	*money*
*per	*through*
percussit	*struck*
perīculōsus	*dangerous*
perit	*dies, perishes:* periit
*perterritus	*terrified*
pervēnit	*reached, arrived at*
*pēs: pedem	*foot, paw*
pessimus	*worst, very bad*
pestis: pestem	*pest, scoundrel*
*petit	*makes for, attacks, seeks:* petīvit
philosophus	*philosopher*
pictor: pictōrem	*painter, artist*
pictūra	*painting, picture*
pingit	*paints*
piscīna	*fish-pond*
pistor: pistōrem	*baker*
*placet	*it pleases, suits*
*plaudit	*applauds, claps:* plausit
plēnus	*full*
plūrimus	*most*
pōculum	*wine-cup*
*poēta	*poet*
pollex: pollicem	*thumb*
Pompēiānus	*Pompeian*
pōns: pontem	*bridge*
*porta	*gate*
*portat	*carries:* portāvit
porticus	*colonnade*
*portus	*harbour*
*post	*after*
posteā	*afterwards*
*postquam	*after, when*
postrēmō	*finally, lastly*
postrīdiē	*on the next day*
*postulat	*demands:* postulāvit
posuit	*placed, put up*
praemium	*profit, reward*
pretiōsus	*expensive, precious*
*prīmus	*first*
probat	*proves*
probus	*honest*
*prōcēdit	*advances, proceeds:* prōcessit
*prōmittit	*promises:* prōmīsit
*prope	*near*
propius	*right, proper*
prōvocāvit	*called out, challenged*

proximus	*nearest*
*puella	*girl*
*puer	*boy*
*pugna	*fight*
*pugnat	*fights:* pugnāvit
*pulcher: pulchrum	*beautiful*
pulcherrimus	*very beautiful*
pulchrior	*more beautiful*
*pulsat	*hits, knocks at, punches:* pulsāvit
pȳramis: pȳramidem	*pyramid*

q

quadrāgintā	*forty*
*quaerit	*searches for, looks for:* quaesīvit
*quam	*than, how*
quam celerrimē	*as quickly as possible*
quantī?	*what price? how much?*
quid?	*what?*
quiētus	*quiet*
quīndecim	*fifteen*
quīnquāgintā	*fifty*
quīnque	*five*
*quis?	*who?*
quō?	*where, where to?*
*quod	*because*
*quoque	*also, too*

r

rapit	*seizes, grabs:* rapuit
recitat	*recites*
recumbit	*lies down, reclines:* recubuit
recūsāvit	*refused*
*reddit	*gives back*
rediit	*went back, came back, returned*
*rēs: rem	*thing*
rem cōgitat	*considers the problem*
rem cōnfēcit	*finished the job*
rem intellegit	*understands the truth*
rem nārrat	*tells the story*
rem probat	*proves the case*

respīrāvit	*recovered breath, recovered consciousness*
*respondet	*replies:* respondit
rētiārius	*net-fighter*
retinet	*holds back, keeps*
*revenit	*comes back, returns*
rhētor: rhētorem	*teacher*
*rīdet	*laughs, smiles:* rīsit
rīdiculus	*ridiculous, silly*
*rogat	*asks:* rogāvit
Rōma	*Rome*
Rōmānus	*Roman*
ruīna	*ruin, wreckage*
ruit	*rushes:* ruit

s

sacrificium	*offering, sacrifice*
*saepe	*often*
salit	*leaps, jumps*
salūs: salūtem	*safety*
*salūtat	*greets:* salūtāvit
*salvē!	*hello!*
*sanguis: sanguinem	*blood*
*satis	*enough*
scaena	*stage, scene*
scissus	*torn*
scit	*knows*
*scrībit	*writes:* scrīpsit
scrīptor: scrīptōrem	*sign-writer*
sculptor: sculptōrem	*sculptor*
scurrīlis	*rude*
secat	*cuts:* secuit
secundus	*second*
*sed	*but*
*sedet	*sits*
sella	*chair*
sēmirutus	*half-collapsed*
sēmisomnus	*half-asleep*
*semper	*always*
*senātor: senātōrem	*senator*
*senex: senem	*old man*
senior	*older, elder*
sēnsim	*slowly, gradually*
sententia	*opinion*
*sentit	*feels:* sēnsit
serpēns: serpentem	*snake*

*servat	*saves, looks after, preserves:* servāvit
*servus	*slave*
sibi	*to himself*
*signum	*sign, seal, signal*
*silva	*wood*
sine	*without*
*sollicitus	*worried, anxious*
*sōlus	*alone, lonely*
sonuit	*sounded*
sonus	*sound, noise*
sordidus	*dirty*
soror: sorōrem	*sister*
*spectāculum	*show, spectacle*
*spectat	*looks at, watches:* spectāvit
spectātor: spectātōrem	*spectator*
spīna	*thorn*
splendidus	*splendid*
*stat	*stands*
*statim	*at once*
statua	*statue*
stēlla	*star*
stertit	*snores*
stilus	*pen, stick*
stola	*dress*
*stultus	*stupid*
stultior	*more stupid*
stultissimus	*very stupid*
suāviter	*sweetly*
*subitō	*suddenly*
*superat	*overcomes, overpowers:* superāvit
superfuit	*survived*
*surgit	*gets up, rises:* surrēxit
suscipit	*undertakes, takes on*
susurrāvit	*whispered, muttered*
*suus	*his, her, their*
Syrius	*Syrian*

t

*taberna	*shop, inn*
tablīnum	*study*
*tacet	*is silent, is quiet:* tacuit
*tacitē	*quietly, silently*
*tamen	*however*
*tandem	*at last*
tantum	*only*
tē	*you (singular)*
tēcum	*with you (singular)*
*templum	*temple*
tenet	*holds*
*terra	*ground, land*
*terret	*frightens:* terruit
tertius	*third*
testis: testem	*witness*
theātrum	*theatre*
thermae	*baths*
tibi	*to you (singular)*
*timet	*is afraid, fears:* timuit
timidē	*nervously*
titulus	*notice, slogan*
toga	*toga*
tondet	*shaves, trims*
tōnsor: tōnsōrem	*barber*
*tōtus	*whole*
*trādit	*hands over:* trādidit
trahit	*drags:* trāxit
tremor: tremōrem	*trembling, tremor*
tremuit	*trembled, shook*
*trēs	*three*
triclīnium	*dining-room*
trīgintā	*thirty*
trīste	*sadly*
trīstis	*sad*
*tū	*you (singular)*
tuba	*trumpet*
*tum	*then*
tunica	*tunic*
*turba	*crowd*
turbulentus	*rowdy, disorderly*
tūtus	*safe*
*tuus	*your, yours*

u

*ubi	*where*
ubīque	*everywhere*
ululāvit	*howled*
umbra	*shadow, ghost*
*ūnus	*one*
*urbs: urbem	*city*
ūtilis	*useful*
ūtilissimus	*very useful*
*uxor: uxōrem	*wife*

v

vāgīvit	*cried, wailed*
*valdē	*very much, very*
*valē	*goodbye*
valedīxit	*said goodbye*
valet	*feels well*
*vehementer	*violently, loudly*
vēnālīcius	*slave-dealer*
vēnātiō:	
vēnātiōnem	*hunt*
*vēndit	*sells*
*venit	*comes:* vēnit
*verberat	*strikes, beats:* verberāvit
versipellis:	
versipellem	*werewolf*
versus	*verse, line of poetry*
vertit	*turned*
vexat	*annoys*
*via	*street*
vibrat	*waves, brandishes*
victor: victōrem	*victor, winner*
*videt	*sees:* vīdit
vīgintī	*twenty*
vīlicus	*farm manager, bailiff*
vīlla	*house, villa*
*vīnum	*wine*
*vir	*man*
vīsitat	*visits*
vīta	*life*

*vituperat	*blames, curses:* vituperāvit
vīvit	*is alive*
vōbīs	*to you (plural)*
*vocat	*calls:* vocāvit
*vōs	*you (plural)*
vulnerāvit	*wounded, injured*